KU-052-783

# Country Cottage Quilting

## Lynette Anderson

D&C
David and Charles

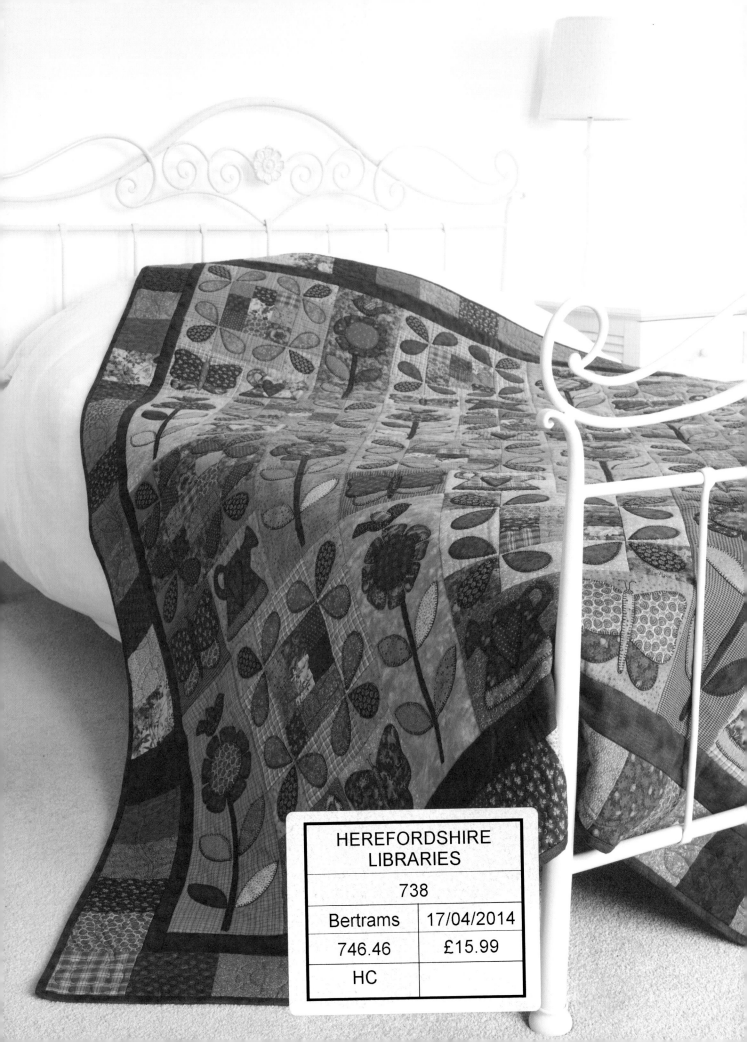

| HEREFORDSHIRE LIBRARIES | |
| --- | --- |
| 738 | |
| Bertrams | 17/04/2014 |
| 746.46 | £15.99 |
| HC | |

# Country Cottage
## Quilting

HC

740006607385

# Contents

# Introduction

*T*hatched cottages and their rambling country gardens are a never-ending source of delight and were my inspiration for all the designs in this book. My love of cottages comes from growing up in an English country village, and the golden thatched roofs and colourful gardens are firmly embedded in my childhood memories.

With these memories in mind I have had great fun making quilts, throws, wall hangings, cushions, pictures, bags and sewing accessories, all with the lovely cottage and garden theme and I hope you will find some wonderful things to inspire you to pick up a needle and thread.

In the Cottage Garden chapter there is a lovely collection of sewing bag, needle case and scissor holder. The designs were inspired by my Aunt June's cottage, whose home was a cosy place – warm in winter with a fire in the hearth and a garden that was a riot of colour in summer.

The Vintage Flowers chapter has a gorgeous quilt and matching cushion in lovely faded antique colours of blues, greys and creams, echoing the calming atmosphere

of times gone by. Sixteen-patch blocks alternate with appliquéd spool blocks, adorned with cheerful flowers and a cheeky bird.

The Birdhouse Garden designs on a handy bag and little coin purse reflect my love of birds and the joy they bring. My mum is a keen gardener and our garden was always filled with many bird-friendly plants. In winter we filled the birdfeeders and cracked the ice in the birdbath so the birds could come for food and water.

In the Walnut Tree Cottage chapter a delightful cottage scene complete with a splendid walnut tree in bloom forms a wonderful design to decorate a really useful sewing case and a little needle holder. Felix the cat snoozes contentedly among the flowers.

The Flowers for the Bees chapter gives thanks for the humble bee, without which our gardens wouldn't exist. A charming wall hanging with a busy hive and towering delphiniums is decorated with appliqué, hand embroidery and yoyos for three-dimensional flowers. The design also appears as a framed picture worked just with hand embroidery.

My Favourite Garden features a lovely quilt decorated with individual garden scenes. The gardens of country cottages were famed for cramming all sorts of details into a small space. These little areas were filled with favourite flowers and well-chosen ornaments, bringing the garden to life. Two little flowerpot pictures are ideal to give as gifts.

The Go Wild Garden chapter celebrates the simple pleasures of a garden – whether it's playing in the mud as a child, rolling in the grass, chasing butterflies or lying under tall sunflowers.

A magnificent quilt in ambers, rusts and blues is made from a block repeated and rearranged to create a design full of interest. A matching pillow using the same patchwork and appliqué block is perfect to cushion your head as you relax under the sun.

The combination of stitchery and appliqué is currently my favourite look and the designs in this book unite those hand skills beautifully. I love attention to detail: this can make my work look complicated but on closer inspection you will see that I only use basic stitches, making my designs achievable for all skill levels.

The patchwork in the designs is straightforward, with easy blocks and useful diagrams. I have used a fusible web method of appliqué and more traditional needle-turn appliqué, and the step-by-step text gives detailed instructions on both of these. You could use either method for the projects in the book. The techniques required are either described within the chapters or in the Techniques section at the back of the book. All the templates you will need are provided in the Templates section. They have been reduced to fit the book but it is easy to take the book to a photocopier and enlarge all the designs for your own use.

So many people adore quaint cottages and country gardens and I'm sure you will love the charming designs in this book – happy stitching!

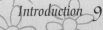

# Cottage Garden

*T*his gorgeous sewing set of bag, needle case and scissor keeper features a sweet thatched cottage and its flower garden. An enjoyable mixture of patchwork, appliqué and embroidery makes them a pleasure to stitch, and great to give as gifts too. You could make the projects individually or work them as a pretty trio.

The simple drawstring bag is the perfect size for your sewing work in progress – just take it along to your sewing group, sit back and wait for it to be admired. I just love the needle case, with its tiny prairie points that set off the stitchery perfectly. There is a place to put your name and the year on the front, while inside there are pockets to safely store needles and threads. A sturdy scissor keeper completes the collection and is the perfect way to keep your scissors safe and easy to find.

# Hollyhock Cottage Bag

This useful bag is so easy to make you'll want to create lots for family and friends.
The threads and stitches used for the little stitchery that adorns the bag are described
at the end of the project.

## You will need...

❀ Two pieces of dark brown print each
5½in x 10in (14cm x 25.4cm)

❀ Two pieces of brown floral each
8½in x 10in (21.5cm x 25.4cm)

❀ Two pieces of brown check for lining
each 10in x 14in (25.4cm x 35.5cm)

❀ Two pieces of blue print for casing
each 2in x 9in (5cm x 23cm)

❀ Cream textured fabric for stitchery
background 6in (15cm) square

❀ Tiny blue check for house appliqué
2in (5cm) square

❀ Scrap of blue print for door appliqué

❀ Ginger wool for roof 2in x 2½in
(5cm x 6.5cm)

❀ Stranded embroidery cotton (floss):
ginger, salmon pink, dirty mauve,
black, aged red, moss green, grey
and petrol blue (I used Cosmo
threads but DMC equivalents are
suggested in the instructions)

❀ Fusible stabilizer (optional)

❀ Fine-tipped fabric marking pen in
brown

❀ Cream cord drawstring 1¾yd (1.5m)

❀ Template plastic

❀ Light box (optional)

❀ Tacking (basting) glue (optional)

**Finished size:**
9½in x 13½in (24.1cm x 34.3cm)

−✕−✕−✕−✕−✕−✕−✕−✕−✕−✕−✕−✕−✕−✕−

# Working the appliqué

**1** Use the relevant templates given in Templates at the back of the book. Using your favourite method of appliqué, prepare the appropriate pieces (see Working Appliqué in the Techniques section). If using needle-turn appliqué, add a seam allowance around the shapes. If using fusible web appliqué, reverse the template shapes before using. I used needle-turn appliqué for this project and made the templates for the appliqué shapes from paper. Once the edges are turned under and tacked (basted), press the shapes, first on the wrong side and then on the right side.

**2** Using the photograph as a guide, position the appliqué shapes. I used a light box, placing the pattern sheet on to the light box and positioning the background fabric on top. If you don't have a light box use a bright window. Once you are happy with the positioning glue tack (baste) or pin the appliqué shapes in place.

**3** Stitch the appliqué shapes in position using a blind hem stitch and thread to match the background fabric so it doesn't show.

**4** Using a fine-tipped fabric marking pen either freehand draw or trace the embroidery lines from the template. Work the stitchery following the instructions at the end of this project.

*Tip*

I use a tacking (basting) glue to fix the shapes in position on the background as I don't like the way thread gets caught around the pins when I'm sewing the shapes into place. Roxanne's Glue Baste It™ has a small tube through which tiny drops of glue emerge, allowing for fine placement of the glue.

## Making the bag

**5** To make up the bag cut the following pieces.
Two pieces 5½in x 10in (14cm x 25.4cm) from dark brown print for the bottom of the bag.
Two pieces 8½in x 10in (21.6cm x 25.4cm) from brown floral for the top of the bag.
Two pieces 10in x 14in (25.4cm x 35.5cm) from brown check for the bag lining.
Two pieces 2in x 9in (5cm x 23cm) from blue floral for the drawstring casing.

**6** Take one top bag piece and one bottom bag piece and join together, pressing the seam open. This is the bag front. Repeat with other two pieces for the back of the bag.

**7** Using the template provided, make a template from template plastic for the large circle. With the wrong side of fabric facing up, centre the circle template over the stitchery. With a fabric marking pen or pencil draw around the template. Cut out on the line (a seam allowance has been included in the template). Turn under about ¼in (6mm) all around the circle, tack (baste) and then press.

**8** Place the bag front piece right side up on a flat surface and using the picture on the previous page as a guide position the stitchery circle. Once you are happy with the position glue or pin in place and then stitch using a blind hem stitch.

**9** Take the two pieces for the drawstring casing and press ¼in (6mm) under on all four sides of both pieces. On a flat surface and with the right side of the bag front and back pieces facing up, centre the drawstring casing about 1¼in (3.2cm) down from the top edge of both pieces **(see Fig 1)**. Stitch the casing in place with hand blanket stitch down the two long sides using two strands of aged red.

**Fig 1**

1¼in
(3.2cm)

Casing

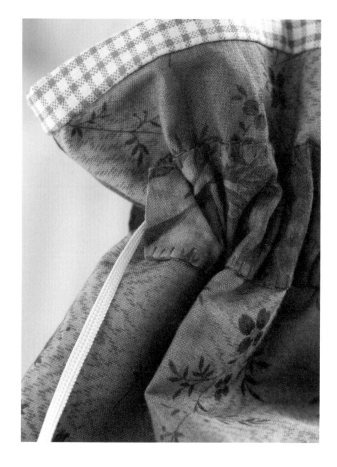

10 Take the bag outer and with right sides together and using a ¼in (6mm) seam allowance stitch around three sides leaving the top open **(Fig 2)**. Take the brown check bag lining pieces cut earlier and with right sides together and a ¼in (6mm) seam allowance, stitch around three sides leaving about 3in (7.6cm) open in one of the sides.

12 Cut the cord in half and starting from the left side of the bag, thread one piece of cord through the front casing and then the back casing. Repeat with the other piece of cord but start from the right side **(Fig 3)**. Finish by tying a knot in the end of each pair of cords so they cannot pull out of the casing when the bag is in use.

**Fig 2**

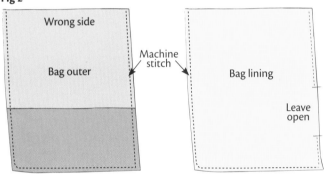

Wrong side

Bag outer

Machine stitch

Bag lining

Leave open

**Fig 3**

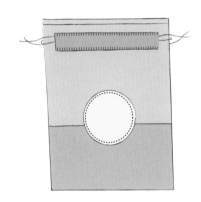

11 With right sides together place the bag inside the lining and stitch along the top edges to join them together making sure you match side seams. Turn the bag through the gap so the right side is now facing outwards and slipstitch the opening closed. Press the bag lightly. Because the lining was cut longer than the outer bag it will fall to the outside, giving a nice contrasting band at the top edge of the bag.

 Tip

Using a large safety pin will help you thread the cord through the casing easily. Place the safety pin into the end of the cord and feed the safety pin into and along the casing. Remove the pin and repeat for the other length of cord.

X—X—X—X—X—X—X—X—X—X—X—X—X—X—

# Working the stitchery

Use the information in the panel below to work the stitcheries on the bag, needle case and scissor keeper. Transfer the stitchery designs on to the right side of the fabric you have chosen for the stitchery background, ensuring that there is plenty of space between each of the designs to cut apart once the stitching has been completed. Once all embroidery is complete press carefully.

I used Cosmo threads but DMC equivalent codes have been suggested below. Two strands of thread were used, unless otherwise stated. See Embroidery Stitches in the Techniques section for how to work the stitches. The stitches used were (abbreviations in brackets): backstitch (BS), blanket stitch (BKS), French knot (FK), lazy daisy (LD), running stitch (RS) and satin stitch (SS). If you want to add names or wording of your own use backstitch. An alphabet template is provided in the Template section.

 **Ginger (DMC 3031)**
Outline wheelbarrow (BS)
Hollyhock stems (BS)
Line under house (BS)
Window frames (BS)
Date (BS)

 **Salmon pink (DMC 224)**
Hollyhocks, left side (BKS)
Dots on flowers on hill (FK)
Centre dots in right-hand hollyhock (FK)

 **Dirty mauve (DMC 317)**
Dots and name on scissor holder (FK & BS)
Name on needle case (BS)
Dashed lines on outer borders (RS)

 **Black (DMC 310)**
Line above wheelbarrow (BS)
Bird legs and beaks (BS)
Bird eyes (FK)
Line above bird on scissor holder (BS)
Scrolls below heart on watering can (BS)
Dashed line under wheelbarrow (RS)

 **Aged red (DMC 221)**
Birds (BS)
All hearts (SS)
Hollyhock closest to house (BKS)
Dots either side of name (FK)
Centre dots on left-hand hollyhock (FK)
Dashed line under top line of garden (RS)

 **Moss green (DMC 730)**
Watering can (BS)
Hollyhock leaves (BS & RS)
Leaves on hill (LD)
Daisy stems (BS)
Daisy leaves (LD)

 **Grey (DMC 646)**
Daisy centres (FK)
Smoke (BS)
Alphabet, single strand (BS)

 **Petrol blue (DMC 924)**
Daisies (LD)
Chimney (BS)

# Hollyhock Needle Case

This delightful needle case is not only decorative but is certain to be well used, with a felt needle holder and small pockets for holding various sewing accessories.

## You will need...

- Dark brown print for case outer 8in x 12in (20.3cm x 30.5cm)
- Brown floral print for lining 8in x 12in (20.3cm x 30.5cm)
- Cream textured print for stitchery 6in x 10in (15.2cm x 25.4cm)
- Tan check for inner pocket 6in x 10in (15.2cm x 25.4cm)
- Two strips of brown floral 1in x 10½in (2.5cm x 26.7cm) for ties
- Dark brown floral for binding 1¼in (3.2cm) wide x area around case
- Scraps of blue, brown and dark brown floral and blue check
- Ginger wool for roof and needle holder 4½in (11.4cm) square
- Double-sided iron-on interfacing 8in x 12in (20.3cm x 30.5cm)
- Stranded embroidery cotton (floss): ginger, salmon pink, dirty mauve, black, aged red, moss green, grey and petrol blue (I used Cosmo threads but DMC equivalents are suggested in the instructions)
- Fusible web
- Fine-tipped fabric marking pen in brown
- Fusible stabilizer (optional)
- Light box (optional)
- Tacking (basting) glue (optional)

**Finished size:**
**4¾in x 6½in (6.5cm x 12cm)**

## Working stitchery and appliqué

1 Use the relevant templates given in Templates at the back of the book. Follow the instructions in the Hollyhock Cottage Bag project to create the appliqué (steps 1–4) and work the stitchery for the exterior and interior of the case. The wheelbarrow on the inside of the case is embroidered in the same way as the wheelbarrow on the outside, with space to add wording of your choice. Gently press your work.

## Making the case

2 Trim the stitchery to 4½in x 6in (11.4cm x 15.2cm). Turn the edges under, tack (baste) in place and press gently. Trim the interior stitchery to 2¾in x 4¾in (7cm x 12cm). Turn the edges under, tack in place and press gently. Place aside for later.

3 From dark brown print cut a piece 6½in x 9½in (16.5cm x 24.1cm) for the case outer. From brown floral print cut a piece 6½in x 9½in (16.5cm x 24.1cm) for the case lining. From tan check cut a piece 5½in x 9½in (14cm x 24.1cm) for the inner pocket. From the ginger wool cut a piece for the needle holder 2¼in x 3¼in (5.7cm x 8.2cm).

4 Press the needle case outer piece in half to become 6½in x 4¾in (16.5cm x 12cm). Position the house stitchery on the front of the case and pin in place (see Fig 1).

**Fig 1**

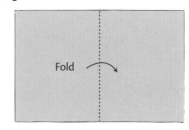

## Making the prairie points

5 Cut ten 1in (2.5cm) squares from assorted fabrics and press into triangles following **Fig 2**.

**Fig 2**

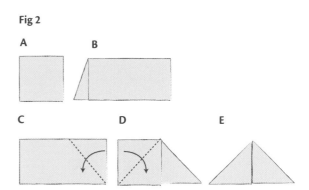

6 Position five prairie points along the top and five along the bottom of the stitchery, with the raw bottom edges of the points under the stitchery. Stitch down using a blind hem stitch.

7 Bond the needle case outer with its stitchery design on to one side of the double-sided adhesive interfacing (I used Pellon Peltex).

## Making the inner pocket

8 Take the 5½in x 9½in (14cm x 24.1cm) pocket piece and fold it in half lengthwise. Press and then divide the left-hand half into three **(Fig 3)** (remembering there will be a ¼in/6mm seam at each end). Press lightly to mark the thirds.

**Fig 3**

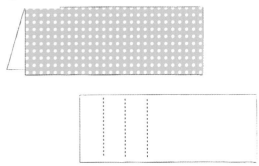

9 Using Fig 4 below, position the inner pocket stitchery and stitch in place.

## Working the appliqué

10 Trace around the heart template three times on to the paper side of fusible web, leaving about ½in (1.3cm) around each heart. Fuse the hearts on the centre of each third of the pocket **(Fig 4)** – remembering that there will be a ¼in (6mm) seam at the bottom of the pocket (see Fusible Web Method in the Techniques section).

**Fig 4**

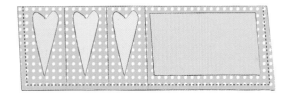

11 When the appliqué is fused into place, use two strands of embroidery thread to work blanket stitch around the edges of the shapes.

## Making the needle case inner

12 Take the needle case lining cut previously and position the pocket, pinning it in. Work a running stitch with two strands of petrol blue stranded cotton on the crease lines of each pocket to divide them.

13 Position the previously cut ginger wool for the needle holder and pin in place. Using two strands of ginger thread work blanket stitch around the edge to hold in place. Gently press your work.

14 Bond the needle case lining with its pockets to the other side of the adhesive interfacing.

## Making the ties

15 Fold one of the tie strips in half lengthwise, right sides together. Machine stitch across one of the short sides and the entire long side. Turn through to the right side. Repeat with other strip.

16 Position the ties facing inwards, aligning raw edges and pin in place **(Fig 5)**. The ties will get stitched into place as you add the binding.

**Fig 5**

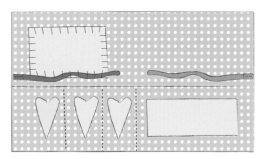

## Binding the case

17 Cut the binding 1¼in (3.2cm) wide on the straight of the grain. Join strips to make the necessary length to go around the case and then press in ¼in (6mm) down the length of the binding. Bind the edge following the directions for Binding in the Techniques section.

# Gardener's Scissor Keeper

This scissor holder is padded with wadding and is perfect for keeping your scissors safe. Personalize the stitchery design by stitching your name above the little bird, either freehand or using the alphabet template at the back of the book.

## You will need...

❀ Dark brown print for back and lining 8in (20.3cm) square

❀ Cream textured fabric for stitchery 5in (12.7cm) square

❀ Fusible stabilizer 5in (12.7cm) square (optional)

❀ Stranded embroidery cotton (floss): ginger, salmon pink, dirty mauve, black, aged red, moss green, grey and petrol blue (I used Cosmo threads but DMC equivalents are suggested in the instructions)

❀ Thin card

❀ Clear, fast-tack craft glue

❀ Thin wadding (batting) or fusible interfacing

❀ Template plastic

❀ Fine-tipped fabric marking pen in brown

❀ Light box (optional)

**Finished size:**
2½in x 4in (6.3cm x 10.2cm)

# Working the stitchery

1 Use the relevant templates given in Templates at the back of the book. Transfer the stitchery design for the scissor keeper on to the right side of the cream textured print, leaving at least 2in (5cm) between the designs to cut them apart later. Follow the instructions at the end of the Hollyhock Cottage Bag for stitching the designs.

# Making the scissor keeper

2 Make templates from template plastic for the two scissor holder shapes. Place the templates on to the wrong side of your stitchery and, making sure that you have centred the stitchery, draw around the template with a pencil. Cut out these shapes, cutting out about ⅜in (1cm) beyond the drawn line to allow for a seam. Use the same templates to mark the shapes on your print backing fabric, cutting out about ⅜in (1cm) beyond the drawn line to allow for a seam.

3 Use the templates to mark the shapes on thin wadding (batting) but this time no seam allowance is needed, so cut out the shapes exactly on the line. Use the templates to mark the shapes on thin card, cutting out the shapes exactly on the line. Cut two card pieces for each shape.

4 Take one card back piece and one card front piece and use fast-tack glue to stick thin wadding on to one side of each of them.

5 Place the stitchery for the front of the scissor keeper wrong side up and place the appropriate card shape on top, wadding side up. Carefully put glue around the edge of the card and then bring the ¼in (6mm) seam allowance over the edge on to the glue **(Fig 1)**. Hold in place while the glue is drying. Do the same for the other piece of stitchery and the back piece of card. Repeat this process with the other pieces of card and the backing fabric pieces. Place these four pieces aside for the moment.

Fig 1

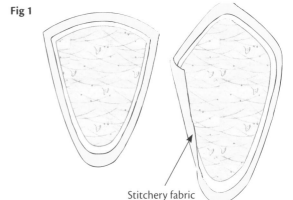

Stitchery fabric folded over and glued in place

 Tip ........................................................

To ensure that the stitchery is centred on the card, hold the stitchery up to bright light with the card shape behind – you will be able to see if you have it in the correct place.

## Making the tassel and cord

**6** To make the tassel, cut a piece of card 1¼in (3.2cm) wide. Cut petrol blue and ginger stranded cotton, each about 30in (76.2cm) long and wrap them around the card about twenty times. Slide the tassel carefully off the card.

**7** To make the cord, take petrol blue and ginger stranded cotton, each about 48in (122cm) long. Anchor one end of the threads under something heavy or ask a friend to hold one end. Twist the threads in a clockwise direction until the cord wants to double back on itself, but don't let it yet! Thread the twisted cord through the top loops of the tassel, centre the tassel on the cord and now let the cord double back on itself. Hold on to the ends while it twists and then tie a knot at the end to secure the cord. Cut through the bottom loops of the tassel. Take a short length of thread and wrap it around the tassel about ¼in (6mm) from the top loop. Secure with a knot and put the thread ends out of sight.

## Assembling the scissor keeper

**8** Take your four pieces of covered card and check that the glue has dried. Place the front pieces wrong sides together and glue together. Repeat the process with the two back pieces but first place the end of the twisted cord in the centre top between the two back pieces. You now have a back and a front for your scissor holder **(Fig 2)**.

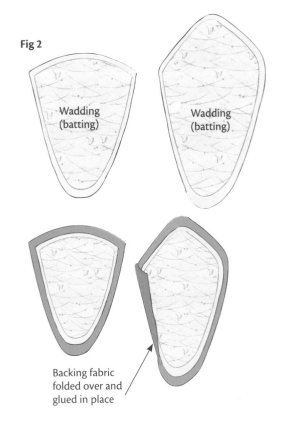

**Fig 2**

Wadding (batting)

Wadding (batting)

Backing fabric folded over and glued in place

♥ *Tip*

You could use washing pegs or bulldog clips to hold the scissor keeper layers together while the glue is drying, to ensure they bond well.

**9** Using two strands of ginger stranded cotton and herringbone stitch, join the front and back pieces together, stitching the seam of the top front edge of the scissor holder **(Fig 3)**. Now join the front to the back, stitching all around the edge to finish the holder.

**Fig 3**

# Vintage Flowers

Faded flowers mixed with antique colours give this lovely quilt and matching cushion a wonderfully vintage feel, although the design could easily be made from brighter contemporary colours. Little birds sitting atop wooden spools with pretty flowers give texture and dimension to the design.

The sixteen-patch blocks in the quilt are made up of squares and are very straightforward to stitch. The placement of light and dark squares also creates a strong diagonal element to the quilt. The spool blocks are a charming combination of needle-turn appliqué, English paper piecing, yoyo flowers and easy stitchery, with the layout of the motifs varied over the quilt to provide added interest.

A cushion project uses the same techniques, plus a plain border decorated with hand quilting, and would be a good way to practise the techniques before beginning on the quilt.

# Flower Spool Quilt

This antique-style quilt uses soft and faded colours. Texture and dimension are created with English paper pieced hexagons and yoyo flowers. A fat eighth is approximately 9in x 22in (22.9cm x 56cm).

## You will need...

- Cream fabric for background 1yd/m
- Twelve blue and twelve pink prints, fat eighth yd/m each
- Aged blue/grey print for appliqué birds 4in x 12in (10.2cm x 30.5cm)
- Soft brown floral for spool tops 8in x 16in (20.3cm x 40cm)
- Turquoise and blue wool for flowers 8in x 12in (20cm x 30.5cm) each
- Mauve print for inner border 6in (15.2cm) (width of fabric)
- Precut hexagons for English paper pieced flowers with ¼in (6mm) sides
- Stranded embroidery cotton (floss) – (I used Cosmo threads but DMC equivalents are given in brackets): soft charcoal (413), vintage brown (611), aged fawn (648), dark antique blue (926) and light antique blue (927)
- Fabric for binding 2½in (6.3cm) wide x 160in (406cm) approx
- Backing fabric 42in x 50in (107cm x 127cm)
- Wadding (batting) 42in x 50in (107cm x 127cm)
- Fusible web
- Template plastic
- Fine-tipped fabric marking pen
- Light box (optional)
- Glue pen (optional)
- Tacking (basting) glue (optional)

**Finished size:**
**41½in x 33½in (105.4cm x 85.1cm)**

## Cutting the squares

**1** From cream background fabric cut thirty-one
4½in squares for the flower spool blocks and
256 1½in (3.8cm) squares for use in the sixteen-patch
blocks. From the blue and pink fabrics cut a total of
256 1½in (3.8cm) squares for use in the sixteen-patch
blocks (about eleven squares from each of the twenty-
four fabrics).

## Making the sixteen-patch blocks

**2** Randomly select your 1½in (3.8cm) squares for
the blocks: you need four blues (A), four pink (B)
and eight cream (C). Using ¼in (6mm) seams join the
squares together as in **Fig 1**. Make thirty-two of these
blocks in total. Each finished block should be 4½in
(11.4cm) square.

**Fig 1**

**A**

| A | C | C | B |
| C | A | B | |
| C | B | A | C |
| B | C | C | A |

**B**

**C**

4½in (11.4cm)

## Making the yoyos

**3** The flower spool blocks are made up of yoyos,
hexagon paper-pieced flowers and appliquéd
flowers, birds and spools. To make the yoyos, make
a template from template plastic using the circle
template supplied in Templates. From assorted blue
prints make about forty-seven yoyos – see Making
Yoyos in Techniques.

## Making the hexagon flowers

**4** Make a template from template plastic (seam
allowance is already included) and use it to cut
six hexagons (petals) and one hexagon (flower centre)
for each flower from assorted blue and pink prints.
You need to make about eleven of these tiny hexagon
flowers. See English Paper Piecing in the Techniques
section. Sew seven hexagons together to create a
seven-piece flower.

## Making the wool flowers

5 Using the turquoise and blue wool and fusible web appliqué, create the wool flowers (see Fusible Web Appliqué in Techniques). Prepare a total of forty flowers from the two wool colours.

## Working the appliqué

6 Using the templates and a needle-turn appliqué method (see Needle-Turn Method in Techniques), cut out and prepare the following: thirty-one spools from your assorted prints; sixty-two spool top/bottoms from the soft brown floral and the aged blue/grey print and about eleven birds. Note that some of these need to be facing right and some facing left.

## Making the flower spool blocks

7 Take the thirty-one 4½in (11.4cm) cream background squares cut earlier and position the spool, bird and the various flowers on the squares. Although the same components were used in these blocks, I used a variety of arrangements within each block. Some blocks have a bird, some don't, which I think makes the quilt looks more interesting. See the main picture opposite for different layout ideas.

8 Once you have decided on the layout for each block, position the appliqué shapes and glue or pin them in place.

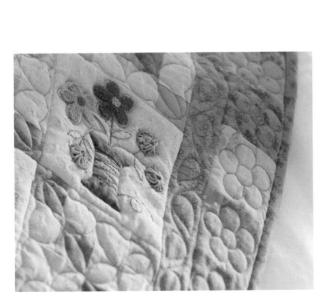

9 Stitch the appliqué shapes in position using blind hem stitch and thread matching the background fabric. Sew the yoyos into place and then add groups of three straight stitches in arrow shapes around the edges, about five around each yoyo, using two strands of light blue (DMC 927) embroidery thread.

10 Using a fine-tipped fabric marking pen either freehand draw or use a light box to trace the lines for the surface embroidery, i.e., the thread on the spool, stems and leaves for the flowers, beaks, wings and eyes on the birds. I used Cosmo threads but DMC equivalents have been given in the You Will Need list. Use two strands of thread for all the embroidery. Work backstitch in brown for the stems and leaves and charcoal for the thread on the spools. Fill the flower centres with French knots in dark blue. Backstitch the birds' wings in fawn. Work the running stitch on the birds' tails in light blue and the beaks in dark blue satin stitch. Stitch a French knot in light blue for the eyes.

## Joining the blocks

11 Using ¼in (6mm) seams join all the blocks together in rows as shown in **Fig 2**, alternating the sixteen-patch blocks with the flower spool blocks. Arrange the blocks so the blue and pink colours in the sixteen-patch blocks run diagonally. Now join the rows together, pinning together carefully so the seams align.

**Fig 2**

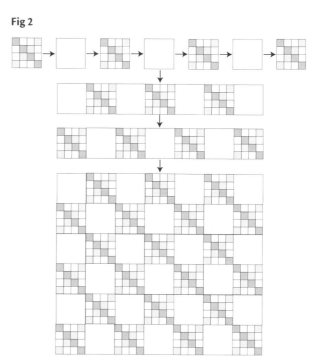

Tip

When sewing the blocks together press the seams in one row of blocks in one direction and the seams in the next row of blocks in the opposite direction. Alternating the pressing this way will help the seams nest together and lie flat when you sew all the rows together.

## Adding the borders

**12** For the inner border, use the mauve print and cut two strips 1½in x 28½in (3.8cm x 72.4cm) for the top and bottom borders. Sew these to the quilt top with ¼in (6mm) seams and press **(Fig 3)**. Cut two strips 1½in x 38½in (3.8cm x 97.8cm) for the side borders. Sew these to the quilt top and press.

**Fig 3**

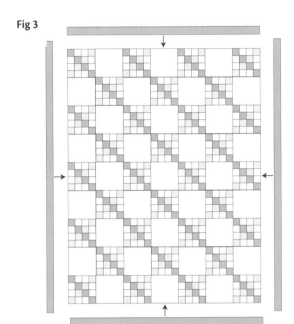

**13** For the outer border, use assorted prints to cut seventy-two 2½in (6.3cm) squares. Select squares at random and join nineteen together. Sew to the side of the quilt and press the seam. Repeat for the other side **(Fig 4)**. Continue selecting squares at random and join seventeen together. Sew to the bottom of the quilt and press the seam. Repeat for the top border.

**Fig 4**

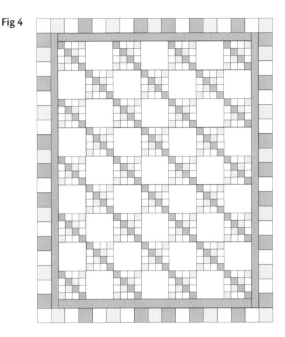

## Quilting and binding

**14** Make a quilt sandwich from the quilt top, wadding (batting) and backing and quilt as desired. I had my quilt professionally longarm quilted by Barb Cowan.

**15** Prepare your binding – I used 2½in (6.3cm) wide double-fold binding but if you want wider or narrow then re-calculate your fabric requirements. Join sufficient strips to go around the quilt – at least 160in (406cm). Bind the quilt following the directions for Binding.

# Flower Spool Cushion

Making a cushion is a great way to practise techniques and try out fabrics before moving on to a larger quilt. This cushion has just one spool block, surrounded by eight sixteen-patch blocks.

## You will need...

❀ Antique cream fabric for background 10in (25.4cm)

❀ Six antique blue prints/florals each 4½in (11.4cm) square

❀ Six antique pink prints/florals each 4½in (11.4cm) square

❀ Aged blue/grey print for appliquéd birds 2in (5cm) square

❀ Soft brown floral for spool tops 2in (5cm) square

❀ Antique blue wool for flower 2in (5cm) square

❀ Stranded embroidery cotton (floss) – (I used Cosmo threads but DMC equivalents are given in brackets): soft charcoal (413), vintage brown (611), aged fawn (648), dark antique blue (926) and light antique blue (927)

❀ Backing fabric 20in (51cm) square

❀ Fusible lightweight wadding (pellon) two pieces 16½in (42cm) square

❀ Toy stuffing or cushion pad

❀ Tacking (basting) glue (optional)

**Finished size:**
**16in (41cm) square**

─✕─✕─✕─✕─✕─✕─✕─✕─✕─✕─✕─✕─✕─✕─

## Making the blocks

**1** From cream background fabric cut one 4½in square for the flower spool block. Cut the blue prints into fifty-four 1½in (3.8cm) squares. Cut the antique pink prints into fifty-four 1½in (3.8cm) squares. This makes a total of 128 squares.

**2** Prepare one flower spool block and eight sixteen-patch blocks, as described in the Flower Spool Quilt. Work the embroidery as described in step 10 of the Flower Spool Quilt. Using ¼in (6mm) seams sew the blocks together in rows and then sew the rows together **(Fig 1)**.

**Fig 2**

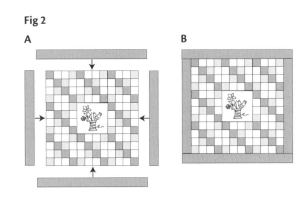

**Fig 1**

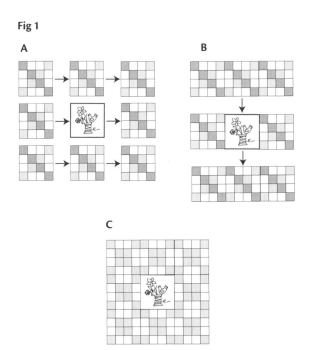

## Adding the border

**3** From antique dark blue floral cut two 2½in x 12½in (6.3cm x 31.7cm) side borders and two 2½in x 16½in (6.3cm x 42cm) top and bottom borders. Using ¼in (6mm) seam allowances sew the side borders to the cushion and press **(Fig 2)**. Sew on the top and bottom borders and press. I hand quilted a curly leaf pattern along the border.

## Assembling the cushion

**4** Cut a 16½in (42cm) square from backing fabric and from lightweight fusible wadding (batting). Following the manufacturer's directions, iron the wadding on to the wrong sides of both the cushion and the backing.

**5** Place the cushion front and back right sides together and stitch around the edge with a ¼in (6mm) seam. Leave a gap of about 4in (10.2cm) in the bottom **(Fig 3)**. Turn the cover through to the right side through the gap, turning out the corners so they are neat and sharp. Press the work gently. Fill the pillow with toy stuffing or use a cushion pad and then stitch up the opening.

**Fig 3**

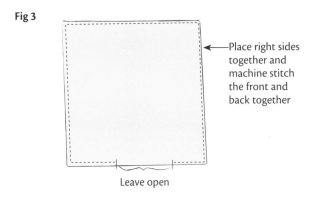

Place right sides together and machine stitch the front and back together

Leave open

# Birdhouse Garden

*A* trip to the market on the weekend requires a bag that's stylish but also not too big and not too heavy and this lovely bag fits the description exactly. It has been created in subtle taupe-coloured fabrics but the design would suit any colour scheme. It has two easy-access front pockets: one is ideal for your sunglasses and features a charming little appliqué and stitchery scene; the other is made from simple patchwork and is a perfect size for your mobile phone. The strap can be made longer or shorter to suit. A neat binding gives the bag a durable edge, while a fabric-covered button with its own little embroidered motif is a lovely finishing touch.

A sweet zippered coin purse makes a great companion for the bag. The little bird stitchery is so adorable it's bound to cause many admiring comments, so you may have to make quite a few for friends and family!

# Birdhouse Bag

This handy lightweight bag has plenty of space and useful pockets. The back is plain, with some simple grid quilting but you could repeat the appliqué and stitchery design, or even create your own design.

## You will need...

- Light beige plaid fabric for outer bag 12in x 20in (30.5cm x 50.8cm)
- Cream floral fabric for lining 12in (30.5cm) (width of fabric)
- Beige fabric for stitchery background 6in x 14in (15.2cm x 35.5cm)
- Plaid fabric for pocket flap and purse backing 6in x 14in (15.2cm x 35.5cm)
- Blue/grey floral and beige/grey floral for pocket 6in (15.2cm) square each
- Scraps of assorted blue, rust and grey prints for appliqué
- Rust wool for birds 3in (7.6cm) square
- Blue/green floral fabric for strap 4in (10.2cm) (width of fabric)
- Small floral print for binding 15in (38cm) square
- DMC stranded embroidery cotton (floss): ecru, black (310), brown (898), soft blue (926), dark blue (3768)
- Two swivel hooks for strap 2in (5cm)
- Iron-on stabilizer (optional)
- Plastic button 1in 2.5cm) diameter
- Iron-on wadding (batting) (I used pellon) 12in (30.5cm)
- Masking tape ½in (1.3cm) wide
- Sewing and quilting threads
- Template plastic
- Fine-tipped fabric marking pen
- Fabric glue

**Finished size:**
**9in x 10in (22.9cm x 25.4cm), excluding strap**

## Working the appliqué

**1** Using the shapes provided in Templates at the back of the book and your favourite method of appliqué, prepare all the appliqué shapes. If you plan to use needle-turn appliqué you will need to add ¼in (6mm) seam allowance to the shapes. If using fusible web appliqué you will need to reverse the shapes before using. I used needle-turn appliqué and made templates for the appliqué shapes from paper. See Working Appliqué in the Techniques section.

**2** From stitchery background fabric cut a piece 4in x 7in (10.2cm x 17.8cm). If you like to work in an embroidery hoop you will need a larger piece of fabric and can trim it to size later. Using the picture as a guide, position the appliqué shapes on the fabric. To make this job easier I used a light box, placing the pattern sheet on to the light box and then positioning the background fabric on top. You can usually see through the fabric well enough to position the shapes. When happy with the positions glue baste or pin the shapes in place. Stitch the appliqué shapes into position using a blind hem stitch, using thread that matches the background fabric so it doesn't show.

## Working the stitchery

**3** Using a light source such as a light box or a window, centre the background fabric right side up over the pattern, lining up the appliquéd shapes. Use a fine-tipped fabric marking pen to trace the stitchery lines. If you can't see though your fabric then draw the stitchery design freehand. If using iron-on stitchery stabilizer iron it on before starting the stitching. Place the shiny side of the stabilizer on the wrong side of the fabric and follow the manufacturer's instructions to bond it in place.

*Tip*

When using traditional appliqué, I use a basting glue to fix the shapes in position on the background. Roxanne's Glue Baste It ™ has a small tube through which tiny drops of glue emerge, allowing for fine placement of the glue. You could use pins but I don't like the way the thread gets caught around the pins when I'm sewing the shapes into place.

4 Work the stitchery using the following stitches and thread colours and the picture on the previous page. Use two strands of embroidery thread unless otherwise stated. The stitches used are backstitch (BS), satin stitch (SS), running stitch (RS), lazy daisy (LD) and French knots (FK). Refer to Embroidery Stitches in Techniques for working the stitches. Numbers below correspond to DMC stranded embroidery threads. Once all the stitching has been completed press your work.

 **Ecru**
Bee's wings (SS)
Centres of all daisies (fill with FKs)
Loose single petals around daisies (LD)
Dashed line under appliquéd hill (RS)

 **Black (310)**
Birds' legs, wings and beaks (BS)
Birds' eyes (FK)
Birds' tail markings (RS)
Alternate stripes on bee's body (SS)
Bee's antennae (BS ending with FK)
Bee trail (RS)
Holes on birdhouses (SS)

 **Brown (898)**
Alternate stripes on bee's body (SS)
Grid on bottom of lower birdhouse (BS)
Rectangles under holes on birdhouses (SS)

 **Soft blue (926)**
Groups of three dots in background (FK)

 **Dark blue (3768)**
Petals on all daisies (SS)

## Making the bag front and back

5 Start by preparing the front and back of the bag, cutting the following pieces.
Two pieces 9in x 10in (22.9cm x 25.4cm) of light beige plaid (bag outer).
Two pieces 10in x 11in (25.4cm x 28cm) of cream floral.
Two pieces 10in x 11in (25.4cm x 28cm) of lightweight iron-on interfacing (bag lining).
One piece 8in x 9in (20.3cm x 22.9cm) of cream floral.
One piece 8in x 9in (20.3cm x 22.9cm) of lightweight iron-on interfacing (pocket lining).

6 Bond the interfacing to the wrong side of all three of the cream floral fabric pieces. Take one of the 10in x 11in (25.4cm x 28cm) cream floral pieces (the back of the bag) and with the interfacing facing up, place the light beige plaid right side up on the interfacing.

7 Work the quilting by placing a strip of ½in (1.3cm) wide masking tape at an angle on the right side of the light beige plaid and using the tape as a guide, machine stitch either side of the tape (**Fig 1A**). Move the tape and repeat (**Fig 1B**), and so on, all across the fabric. Use the tape again as a guide to machine quilt the cross grid (**Fig 1C**). Repeat on the other 10in x 11in (25.4cm x 28cm) cream floral piece (the front of the bag). When the quilting has been completed trim both these pieces down to 9in (22.9cm) wide by 10in (24.5cm) high.

**Fig 1**

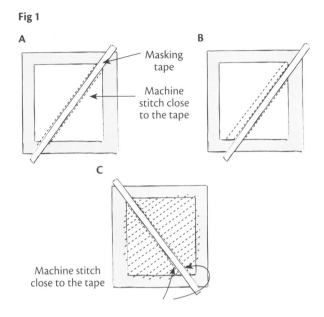

A

Masking tape

Machine stitch close to the tape

B

C

Machine stitch close to the tape

**Fig 3**

A

| Appliqué/ stitchery pocket | Patchwork pocket |

B

7in (17.8cm)

9in (22.9cm)

8   Make the corner curve template from template plastic. Carefully trace around the corner template on the bottom corners of both bag pieces. Cut off the excess fabric with sharp scissors.

## Making the patchwork pocket

9   Make the three templates (1, 2 and 3) for the front of the pocket from template plastic (seam allowance is *not* included in the templates). From selected fabrics cut the pieces out allowing a ¼in (6mm) seam allowance and join the pieces together **(Fig 2)**. Now join the appliqué pocket and the patchwork pocket together **(Fig 3)**.

10   Bond the interfacing to the wrong side of the cream floral fabric. Place the joined pocket piece wrong side down on the interfacing. Pin the layers together if required. Machine quilt the pocket front (see picture as a guide). Rather than drawing the quilting lines on to the fabric I used masking tape for a guide, as before.

**Fig 2**

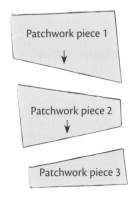

Patchwork piece 1

↓

Patchwork piece 2

↓

Patchwork piece 3

## Binding the pockets

**11** Only the top edge of the combined pocket needs to be bound. From the small floral print prepare some bias binding. Bias binding is made from fabric strips cut on the cross grain (bias) direction of the fabric. Cutting bias strips makes the fabric more flexible and easier to shape. Take the fabric and fold it in half diagonally **(Fig 4)**. Open out the fabric and cut strips on the cross grain. For this project I cut my strips 1¼in (3.2cm) wide and joined them to make a total length of about 60in (152.5cm). Fold and press about ¼in (6mm) of fabric in along the entire length, wrong sides together.

**12** With the pocket front facing up and with right sides together, place the raw edge of the binding on the top edge of the pocket. Pin and machine stitch into place using a ¼in (6mm) seam. Turn the pressed edge of the binding to the back of the pocket and slipstitch into place – it should just cover the line of machine stitching. (See Binding in Techniques for more advice.)

**13** Carefully trace around the corner template on the wrong side of the bottom corners of the pocket piece. Cut off the excess fabric. Take the previously quilted bag front and the quilted front pocket, place them together and carefully machine stitch the pocket to the bag front, down the line between the two pockets **(Fig 5)**.

**Fig 4**

A

Square of fabric

B

Fold diagonally

C

Open out and cut strips on the cross grain at the desired width

**Fig 5**

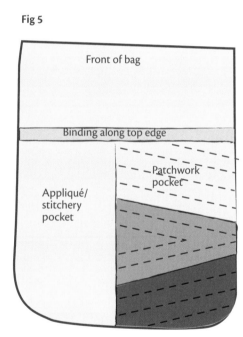

Front of bag

Binding along top edge

Appliqué/ stitchery pocket

Patchwork pocket

**Tip**

You could make the bias binding for the Little Bird Purse at the same time as the bag binding. If you do, you need to allow about 20in (50.8cm) of extra binding for the purse.

## Making the pocket flap

**14** Using the templates, cut a paper template for the pocket flap. Fold a piece of the plaid fabric in half, right sides together and draw around the template with a suitable fabric marking pen **(Fig 6)**. Machine stitch on the line, leaving a small opening for turning through to the right side. Cut out about ¼in (6mm) beyond the stitched line, clip curves and remove corners before turning the flap through to the right side. Press gently and then stitch the opening closed. Using the picture as a guide, position the pocket flap on the front of the bag and machine stitch into place.

## Creating the button

**15** Trace and stitch one daisy to the centre of a 2in (5cm) square of background stitchery fabric. If you are using an iron-on stabilizer, iron it on to the fabric before starting the stitching. Stitch the daisy to match the daisies on the pocket. Press the finished stitching gently.

**16** On the wrong side, trace around the plastic button and cut out about ⅜in (1cm) beyond the drawn line. Stitch a row of gathering stitches around the circle and draw up the stitches so the fabric fits tightly around the button. Fasten the thread securely. Stitch the covered button to the centre of the pocket flap.

## Making the strap loops and strap

**17** For the strap loops cut a strip 1in x 7in (2.5cm x 17.8cm) from plaid fabric. With right sides together fold in half lengthways and stitch with a ¼in (6mm) seam **(Fig 7)**. Turn through to the right side. Cut in half and press to form two loops. Fold each loop in half. Take the previously quilted bag back and pin the folded loops in position, pointing inwards, about 1in (2.5cm) from the top edge of the bag. Machine stitch in place.

**Fig 6**

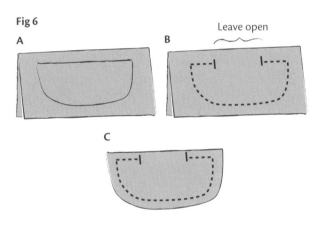

**Fig 7**

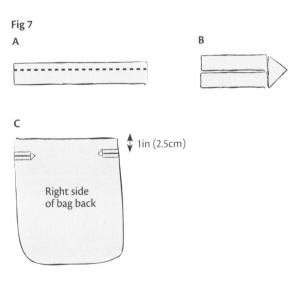

18 Take the bag back and front and with wrong sides together, pin them together, matching corners. Using the bias binding previously made attach the binding around the sides and bottom of the bag in the same way you did to the top edge of the pocket. Now bind the top edge of the bag.

19 For the straps, cut two strips of blue/green floral 1¼in (3.2cm) wide x about 44in (111.7cm) long. Cut a strip of lightweight iron-on interfacing the same size. Bond the interfacing to the wrong side of one of the blue/green floral strips. With right sides together, machine stitch down both sides of the strip **(Fig 8)**. Turn to the right side. Press and then add a row of top stitching on either side for strength and decoration. Finish by attaching a swivel hook to each end of the strap by taking the end of the strap through the swivel hook and hand stitching in place **(Fig 9)**.

**Fig 8**

A  1¼in (3.2cm)  Wrong side of fabric

Machine stitch the layers together with ¼in (6mm) seam allowance

B  ¾in (2cm)

**Fig 9**

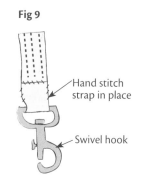

Hand stitch strap in place

Swivel hook

# Little Bird Purse

This dear little purse is easy to make and would make a perfect present for a friend. Find a pretty zip decoration for a lovely finishing touch and add a few shiny coins for luck.

## You will need...

❀ Light beige plaid fabric 5½in x 7in(14cm x 17.8cm)

❀ Beige stitchery background fabric 4in x 6in (10.2cm x 15.2cm)

❀ Cream floral lining fabric 5½in x 7in (14cm x 17.8cm)

❀ Fabric for binding 7in (17.8cm) square

❀ Lightweight iron-on wadding (batting) (I used pellon)

❀ Zip 6in (15.2cm) long

❀ Template plastic

❀ Masking tape ½in (1.3cm) wide, for quilting guide

❀ Fine-tipped fabric marking pen

❀ Light box (optional)

❀ Fabric glue (Roxanne's Glue Baste It™ – optional)

**Finished size:**
**4½in x 3in (11.4cm x 7.6cm) approx.**

## Preparing the stitchery

1 Use the shapes provided in the Templates section at the back of the book. From template plastic make templates for sections A and B of the purse. Trace around template A on to the beige stitchery background fabric and cut out on the line (the seam allowance has been included in the template). Trace around template B on the plaid fabric and cut out on the line (seam allowance is included). Join pieces A and B together **(Fig 1)**.

**Fig 1**

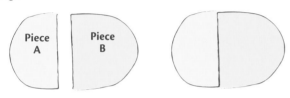

## Working the appliqué

2 Using the picture as a guide and the relevant template, apply the appliqué shapes and then transfer the stitchery (surface embroidery) lines ready for stitching. See steps 2–5 of the Birdhouse Bag for details on working the appliqué and the embroidery stitches. When all the stitching is completed gently press the piece.

## Making up the purse

3 Cut a piece of iron-on wadding (pellon) and a piece of cream floral lining fabric about 5½in x 7in (14cm x 17.8cm). Bond the iron-on wadding to the wrong side of the lining fabric. Place the stitched purse outer right side up on the wadding. Machine quilt using ½in (1.3cm) wide masking tape as a guide, as in step 7 of the Birdhouse Bag **(Fig 2)**. Once the quilting is complete trim the wadding and lining to the same size as the stitched purse outer.

**Fig 2**

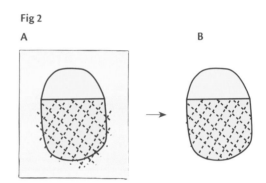

4 Prepare bias binding as for step 11 of the Birdhouse Bag and join the strips to make a total length of about 20in (50.8cm). Bind all around the edge of the oval.

Tip
When adding binding to a curve pin it well and stitch slowly, following the curve closely. Because the binding has been prepared with bias strips it will have enough stretch to curve quite easily.

# Inserting the zip

5 With right sides together and matching the top curve of the purse, check the length of the zip and mark with a pin where it will start and stop **(Fig 3A)**. Hand stitch the side of the purse together, and then repeat for other side **(Fig 3B)**. Carefully place the zip in position and using backstitch stitch it into place, first on one side and then the other **(Fig 3C)**. To make the inside of the purse neat, stitch the selvedge side of the zip carefully to the lining of the purse **(Fig 4)**.

6 To make a nice bottom to the purse, fold and machine stitch across the corner on both sides **(Fig 4)**. Turn the coin purse to the right side and enjoy!

Fig 4

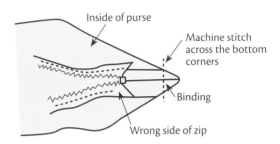

Inside of purse

Machine stitch across the bottom corners

Binding

Wrong side of zip

Fig 3

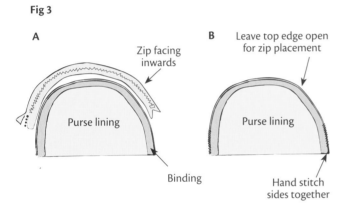

A

Zip facing inwards

Purse lining

Binding

B

Leave top edge open for zip placement

Purse lining

Hand stitch sides together

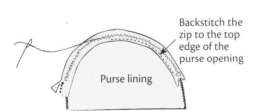

C

Backstitch the zip to the top edge of the purse opening

Purse lining

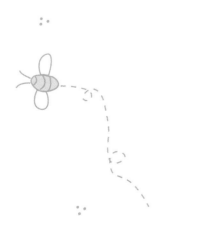

# Walnut Tree Cottage

For the two projects in this chapter I've imagined a spring garden, with a sweet cottage perched on a hill. A walnut tree in bloom promises a bumper harvest of nuts in autumn. A pre-made craft supply case makes a really useful sewing case and looks beautiful once the appliqué and stitchery design is attached. The cottage is created with needle-turn appliqué, with fusible web appliqué used for the roof, which is made from wool to mimic the thatch. Additional surface stitching emulates the thatcher's mesh. A selection of simple hand embroidery stitches makes this project interesting for all levels of stitcher. The back pocket is covered with hexagons, which have been made using traditional English paper piecing.

There is also an ideal companion project for the case in the shape of a needle holder, decorated with a little cottage and some spring flowers.

# Walnut Tree Sewing Case

This case is perfect for all your sewing paraphernalia. I used a ready-to-cover case (available from Lynette Anderson Designs – see Suppliers), which is rigid and has various compartments inside for storing equipment.

## You will need...

❀ Linen-look cream fabric for stitchery background 7¾in x 11¾in (20cm x 30cm)

❀ Green floral fabric for hill appliqué 2in x 11¾in (5cm x 30cm)

❀ Blue print for house appliqué 2½in x 4¾in (6.3cm x 12cm)

❀ Brown wool for thatched roof 2in x 4in (5cm x 10.2cm)

❀ Assorted prints for hexagons, twenty-one 2½in (6.4cm) squares

❀ Stranded embroidery cotton (floss): old gold, bark brown, aged red, soft mauve, charcoal, moss green, eggplant and soft blue (I used Cosmo threads but DMC equivalents have been suggested in the instructions)

❀ Hexagon pre-cut papers with ¼in (6mm) sides

❀ Ready-to-cover sewing case

❀ Fine-tipped fabric marking pen

❀ Sewing and quilting threads

❀ Small curved needle

❀ Template plastic

❀ Iron-on stabilizer (optional)

❀ Light box (optional)

**Finished size:**
9½in x 6in (24.1cm x 15.2cm)

## Transferring the stitchery design

1 Use the shapes provided in the Template section at the back of the book. Using a light source such as a light box or a bright window, centre the cream background fabric right side up over the pattern and use a fine-tipped fabric marking pen to carefully trace all the stitchery lines. If you are using an iron-on stitchery stabilizer iron it on before starting the stitching. Place the shiny side of the stabilizer on to the wrong side of your fabric and follow the manufacturer's instructions to bond it in place with an iron.

**Tip** When choosing the wool for the appliqué roof make sure the weave is not too open or it may fray over time – a nice felted piece will be dense enough and look good.

## Working the appliqué

2 Using the shapes provided in the Template section and your favourite method of appliqué, prepare the hill, cottage and door. If you plan to use needle-turn appliqué you will need to add ¼in (6mm) seam allowance to the shapes. If using fusible web appliqué you will need to reverse the shapes before using. I used needle-turn appliqué for the cottage and door and made templates for the appliqué shapes from paper. See Working Appliqué in the Techniques section.

3 Using the picture as a guide, position the appliqué shapes and then glue baste or pin them in place. I used a light box to help position them and Roxanne's Glue Baste It™, which has a nozzle that allows for fine placement of the glue.

4 Add the thatched roof appliqué. This is made from wool so was applied using fusible web (see Fusible Web Method).

5 Stitch the hill, house and door appliqué shapes in position with blind hem stitch, using a thread that matches the background fabric. For the roof, use two strands of dark brown embroidery thread and blanket stitch around the edge.

# Working the stitchery

**6** Work the stitchery using the following stitches and thread colours. Refer to the picture here and on the previous page. Use two strands of embroidery thread unless otherwise stated. I used Cosmo threads but DMC equivalent codes have been suggested below. The stitches used are backstitch (BS), blanket stitch (BKS), cross stitch (CS), French knots (FK), herringbone stitch (HS), lazy daisy (LD), running stitch (RS) and satin stitch (SS). Refer to Embroidery Stitches in Techniques for working the stitches. When all the stitching is finished press your work.

 **Old gold (DMC 782)**
Daisy centres (fill with FK)
Hollyhock centres (FK)

 **Bark brown (DMC 938)**
Markings on roof (BS, CS & RS)
Birdhouse (BS)
Tree trunk and branches (BS)
Hollyhock stems (BS)
Daisy stems (BS)
Dashed line under top line of hill (RS)

 **Aged red (DMC 221)**
Birds (BS)
Heart on front door (SS)
Chimney pots (SS)
Cat's bell on collar (SS)

 **Soft mauve (DMC 3041)**
Blossom on tree (FK in groups of three)
Cat's collar (SS)
Petals on two of the daisies (SS)

 **Charcoal (DMC 413)**
Window frames (BS)
Cat (BS)
Cat's eyes, nose, mouth (BS, one strand)
Tag for cat's bell (BS)
Hole on birdhouse (SS)
Bird's legs and beaks (BS)
Bird's eyes (FK)

 **Moss green (DMC 3011)**
Hollyhock leaves (BS & RS)
Daisy leaves (BS)
Leaves on tree (LD)

 **Eggplant (DMC 3834)**
Hollyhocks far left (BKS in a circle)
Petals on one of the daisies (SS)

 **Soft blue (DMC 932)**
Hollyhocks near house (BKS in a circle)
Chimney stacks (SS)

## Making the back of the case

**7** The back of the case is made from hexagons. Prepare paper templates and then join twenty-one together **(see Fig 1)** using English Paper Piecing, described in Techniques.

**Fig 1**

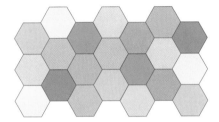

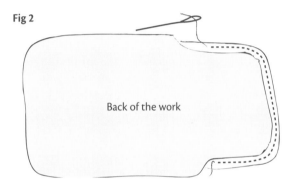

*Tip*

When stitching the deisn in place on the case it took me a little while to get used to using a curved needle, but if you go slowly it's not as hard as you think. A curved needle is very useful for sewing in awkward places.

**8** From template plastic cut templates of the two rectangles for the front and back of the sewing case. Centre the large rectangle template on the stitchery design (front) and cut out with a ¼in (6mm) seam allowance. Repeat with the smaller rectangle and the joined hexagons. Turn under a ¼in (6mm) seam allowance and tack (baste) in place **(Fig 2)**. Press the work lightly. Carefully position the pieces on the front and the back of the sewing case, pinning in place. Stitch the stitchery design in place using a curved needle. Do the same for the hexagons on the back to finish the case.

**Fig 2**

Back of the work

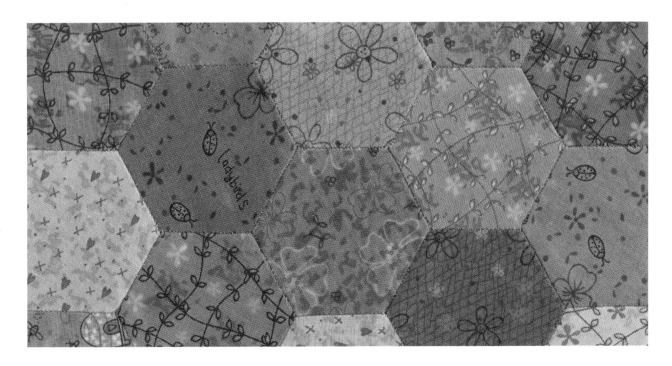

# Cottage Needle Holder

Simple and sweet, this quick-to-make needle holder is ideal for taking out and about with you in your sewing case. It has two wool 'pages' but you could add more.

## You will need...

- ❁ Cream linen-look fabric for stitchery background 4¾in x 8½in (12cm x 21.6cm)
- ❁ Mauve floral fabric for lining 4¾in x 8½in (12cm x 21.6cm)
- ❁ Green floral fabric for hill appliqué 2in x 8½in (5cm x 21.6cm)
- ❁ Blue print fabric for house appliqué 2½in x 4¾in (6.4cm x 12cm)
- ❁ Brown wool for roof appliqué 2in x 4in (5cm x 10.2cm)
- ❁ Cream wool for needle holder 'pages' 4¾in x 8½in (12cm x 21.6cm)
- ❁ Stranded embroidery cotton (floss): old gold, bark brown, aged red, soft mauve, charcoal, moss green, cream, eggplant and soft blue (I used Cosmo threads but DMC equivalents have been suggested in the instructions)
- ❁ Fine-tipped fabric marking pen
- ❁ Iron-on stitchery stabilizer (optional)
- ❁ Light box (optional)

**Finished size:**
**4in (10.2cm) square (when closed)**

## Transferring the stitchery design

1 Use the relevant shapes provided in the Template section at the back of the book. Using a light source such as a light box or a bright window, centre the cream background fabric right side up over the pattern and use a fine-tipped fabric marking pen to carefully trace all the stitchery lines – brown is a useful colour as most stitching will cover this. If you are using an iron-on stitchery stabilizer iron it on before starting the stitching. Place the shiny side of the stabilizer on to the wrong side of your fabric and follow the manufacturer's instructions to bond it in place with an iron.

## Working the appliqué

2 Using the shapes provided in the template section and your favourite method of appliqué, prepare the hill, cottage and door. If you plan to use needle-turn appliqué you will need to add ¼in (6mm) seam allowance to the shapes. If using fusible web appliqué you will need to reverse the template shapes before using them. I used needle-turn appliqué and made templates for the appliqué shapes from paper. See Working Appliqué in the Techniques section.

3 Using the picture as a guide, position the appliqué shapes and then glue baste or pin the shapes in place. I used a light box to help position the shapes and Roxanne's Glue Baste It ™, which has a nozzle that allows for fine placement of the glue.

4 Add the thatched roof appliqué. This is made from wool and doesn't fray so was applied using the fusible web method of appliqué (see Fusible Web Method).

5 Stitch the hill, house and door appliqué shapes into position with a blind hem stitch, using a thread that matches the background fabric so it doesn't show. For the roof, use two strands of dark brown embroidery thread and blanket stitch all around the edge.

**Tip**

Be gentle when pressing your work after the embroidery has been added, so you don't flatten the stitches, especially French knots. Pressing face down on a thick towel will help.

# Working the stitchery

**6** Work the stitchery using the following stitches and thread colours. Use two strands of embroidery thread unless otherwise stated. I used Cosmo threads but DMC equivalent codes have been suggested below. The stitches used are backstitch (BS), cross stitch (CS), French knots (FK), lazy daisy (LD), running stitch (RS) and satin stitch (SS). Refer to Embroidery Stitches in Techniques for working the stitches. Once all the stitching has been completed press your work.

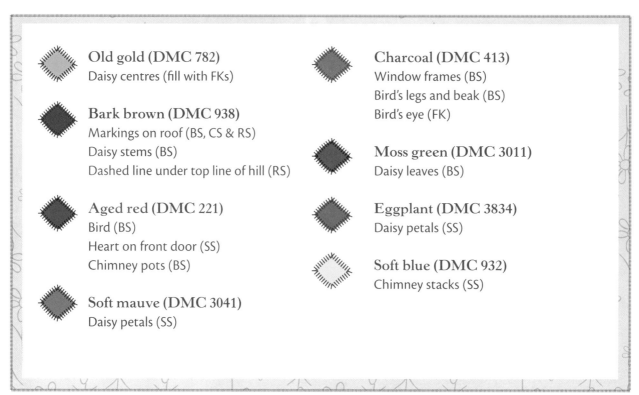

**Old gold (DMC 782)**
Daisy centres (fill with FKs)

**Bark brown (DMC 938)**
Markings on roof (BS, CS & RS)
Daisy stems (BS)
Dashed line under top line of hill (RS)

**Aged red (DMC 221)**
Bird (BS)
Heart on front door (SS)
Chimney pots (BS)

**Soft mauve (DMC 3041)**
Daisy petals (SS)

**Charcoal (DMC 413)**
Window frames (BS)
Bird's legs and beak (BS)
Bird's eye (FK)

**Moss green (DMC 3011)**
Daisy leaves (BS)

**Eggplant (DMC 3834)**
Daisy petals (SS)

**Soft blue (DMC 932)**
Chimney stacks (SS)

## Making up the needle holder

7 Take the stitchery front and the piece of lining fabric and with right sides facing pin the two pieces together. Machine stitch around the needle holder, leaving a small opening for turning through to the right side **(Fig 1)**. Clip the corners before turning the holder to the right side, making sure the corners are nicely turned out and pointed. Press the seam carefully, turning the fabric edges in along the gap. Slipstitch the opening closed and then press the needle holder in half.

8 From cream wool cut a piece 3¼in x 7in (8.2cm x 17.8cm). Centre the piece inside the needle holder. With two strands of cream embroidery thread, sew a running stitch down the centre, making sure you stitch through all layers **(Fig 2)**.

**Fig 2**

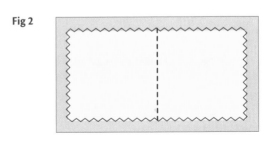

**Fig 1**

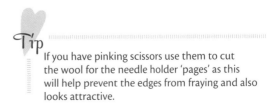

Machine stitching

Wrong side of fabric

Leave small opening

Clip off corners before turning to the right side

Tip

If you have pinking scissors use them to cut the wool for the needle holder 'pages' as this will help prevent the edges from fraying and also looks attractive.

# Flowers for the Bees

*C*ottage gardens are a haven for wildlife, and bees and ladybirds are busy in this sheltered garden where delphiniums tower above the beehive. The techniques used for the wall hanging are easy to do and create a lovely scene. Simple piecing forms the background, which is surrounded by a border of little squares and an outer border made with mitred pieces. Fusible web appliqué is used to create the daisies, bees and hive, with a little ladybird button nestling amongst the flowers. Assorted sizes of yoyos have been used to make the delphiniums, while some surface embroidery ties all the elements together.

If you enjoy hand embroidery you'll love the second project, which is a beehive picture stitched on mottled fabric. The embroidery is given a lovely tactile quality with little buttons decorating the daisy centres and tiny ladybird buttons dotted among the flowers.

# Busy Bees Wall Hanging

This delightful wall hanging is such fun to make. A vaguely green background fabric was used but a warm cream-on-cream would also look good.

## You will need…

* Background: one print 13¾in (35cm) (width of fabric) and three different prints 8in (20.3cm) each (width of fabric)
* Four different tone-on-tone fabrics for borders 10in (25.4cm) each
* Scraps of seven different yellows for beehive and brown for door
* Ten different mauves for delphiniums, largest about 5in (12.7cm) square
* Scraps of cream-on-cream fabric for bees' wings and black for bodies
* Cream-on-cream fabric for daisies 4in (10.2cm) (width of fabric)
* Two green fabrics for leaves, 4in (10.2cm) square each
* Red fabric for pot 6in (15.2cm) square
* Fabric for cat's body 8in (20.3cm) square and two different scraps
* Wood-effect print for post 6in (15.2cm) square
* Wadding (batting) about 27in x 32in (68.6cm x 81.3cm)
* Backing fabric about 27in x 32in (68.6cm x 81.3cm)
* Binding fabric 1½in x 118in (3.8cm x 300cm)
* Two buttons for cat's eyes, one for door handle, six for daisies and two ladybirds
* Fusible web 20in (51cm)
* Stranded embroidery cotton (floss) to match fabrics and perle cotton No.5 in greenish-brown
* Template plastic

**Finished size:**
**25in x 29½in (63.5cm x 75cm)**

## Making the background

1 Take the four background fabrics and cut the following pieces.
A – one piece 7½in wide x 21½in long (19cm x 54.6cm).
B – one piece 10½in wide x 6½in long (26.7cm x 16.5cm).
C – one piece 10½in (26.7cm) square.
D – one piece 10½in wide x 5½in long (26.7cm x 14cm).
Join the pieces together as shown in **Fig 1**, using ¼in (6mm) seam allowances. Press the seams.

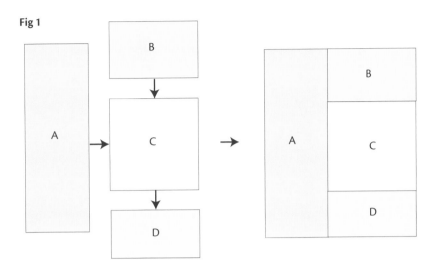

**Fig 1**

## Making the yoyos

2 The delphimium flowers are created from different sized yoyos. Using the shapes provided in Templates at the back of the book, make templates of each of the circles from template plastic. Follow the instructions in Techniques for Making Yoyos. Make about twenty-six in various sizes and set them aside for the moment.

*Tip*
You could use an appliqué mat for this project. One advantage of a mat is that you can iron some of the underneath pieces in place, which allows you to position the top layers with ease. You can remove and re-position fabrics fused to an appliqué mat, but not fabrics already fused to fabrics. See Appliqué Mat Method in Techniques.

## Working the appliqué

**3** Using the templates provided and the Fusible Web Method, apply the beehive, flowerpot, signpost, flowers, leaves and cat. Use two strands of stranded cotton to work blanket stitch around the edges of the appliqués, in colours to match or contrast with the fabrics.

**4** When all blanket stitching has been completed position the yoyos to make the delphiniums, attaching them with blind hem stitch and building from large at the base to small at the top. Using two strands of green stranded cotton add pairs of straight stitches at intervals around each yoyo.

**5** Using the Fusible Web Method, appliqué the bees into position. Work the bees' trails with a black running stitch. Backstitch the antennae in black with a French knot at each end.

## Adding embroidery and buttons

**6** Stitch the rest of the embroidery (see Embroidery Stitches in Techniques). Work the daisy stems in light green chain stitch and backstitch the tendrils in dark green with a French knot on the end. Outline the cat's eyes with fawn backstitch, satin stitch her nose and backstitch her mouth. Take a pencil and draw freehand the vine growing from the flowerpot (or use the template). Use perle No.5 thread to chain stitch the vine in light brown. You could use the alphabet template to create your own wording on the sign. Backstitch the letters in brown with French knots at the letter ends. Trim the centre panel to 16½in x 20½in (42cm x 52cm).

**7** Using matching thread stitch all the buttons in place – in the cat's eyes, centres of the daisy flowers, beehive door and ladybird button.

## Making the pieced border

**8** From each of the four border fabrics cut two 1½in (3.8cm) wide strips across the fabric width (remove selvedges). Pair up the brown/green and yellow/mauve and with right sides facing sew together along the length, to give two 2½in (6.3cm) wide strips from each combination **(Fig 2)**. Press seams. Re-cut the strips to give thirty-eight 1½in x 2½in (3.8cm x 6.3cm) units from the brown/green combination and thirty-eight from the yellow/mauve.

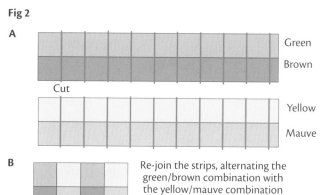

**Fig 2**

A — Green / Brown

Cut

Yellow / Mauve

B — Re-join the strips, alternating the green/brown combination with the yellow/mauve combination

9 Alternating the colour combinations join sixteen of the units together for a top border and then repeat for the bottom border. Sew these borders to the centre panel using ¼in (6mm) seams **(Fig 3)**.

10 Now join twenty-four of the units together for the side borders (you will have to change the corner colours to get the pattern to match around the centre). Sew these borders to the centre panel and press the seams **(Fig 3)**.

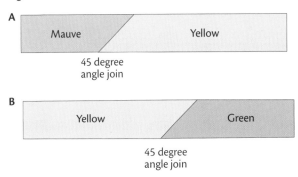

**Fig 4**

A

45 degree angle join

B

45 degree angle join

**Fig 3**

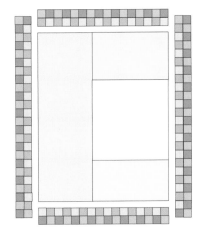

13 With the right side of the fabric facing, cut the right-hand end of the yellow at a 45 degree angle and the left-hand side of the green at a 45 degree angle **(Fig 4B)**. Leave the other ends straight at this time. Join the yellow and green pieces together with a ¼in (6mm) seam. This will be the left side border. Use a green strip for the right-hand side of the border and a brown strip for the bottom **(Fig 5)**. Using ¼in (6mm) seams, join the borders to the appropriate sides. When stitching borders on to the centre panel stitch to within ¼in (6mm) of each end.

## Making the outer border

11 From the mauve, yellow and brown border fabrics cut strips 3½in (8.9cm) wide across the width of the fabric. Remove the selvedges. Cut the yellow strip in half to give two pieces 3½in x 22in (8.9cm x 55.9cm).

12 From the green border fabric cut two pieces 3½in (8.9cm) wide across the width of the fabric. Remove the selvedges. With the right side of the fabric facing, cut the right-hand end of the mauve at a 45 degree angle and the left-hand side of the yellow at a 45 degree angle **(see Fig 4A)**. Leave the other ends straight at this time. Join the mauve and yellow pieces together with a ¼in (6mm) seam. This will be the top outer border.

**Fig 5**

**14** To mitre the corners of the border, take the quilt top to your ironing board. Working on one corner at a time, lay out the un-sewn border ends so they are straight, overlapping the top border with the side border. Lift up the side border and fold it under itself at a 45 degree angle. Make sure that the overlapping fabric lines up with the top border (**Fig 6**). Press a crease, which will be your stitching line. Pin on the angle. Turn the quilt top to the wrong side and stitch along the pinned crease, making sure that you stitch to the corner stitches, which will avoid leaving a gap. Trim away excess fabric and press well. Repeat on the other corners.

**Fig 6**

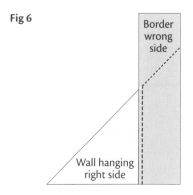

Border wrong side

Wall hanging right side

## Quilting

**15** Cut the backing and wadding (batting) pieces larger than the wall hanging and make a quilt sandwich, as described in Techiques. Depending on whether you are going to hand quilt or machine quilt, tack (baste) or pin layers together accordingly. Quilt as desired. I free-motion quilted a meandering pattern in the background of the central panel and a flower pattern in the outer border. Machine quilting was also worked in the ditch around the inner border and around all of the appliqués.

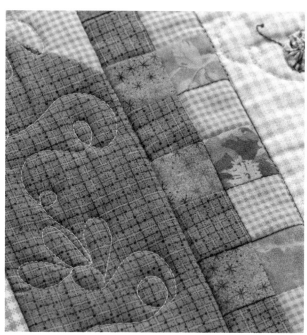

## Binding and finishing

**16** To bind the wall hanging cut a strip 1½in (3.8cm) wide x the necessary length (about 118in (300cm), cut on the straight grain. Press in ¼in (6mm) down the length of the strip. Bind the wall hanging following the instructions for Binding in the Techniques section. Press the finished binding and then label your quilt to finish, if desired – see Labelling Your Quilt.

# Beehive Picture

In this charming framed picture Felix sits contentedly amongst the delphiniums and daisies. This delightful stitchery uses a variety of simple embroidery stitches, with added buttons to give dimension to the scene. You could stitch the bees or use buttons instead and perhaps add a ladybird somewhere in the garden.

## You will need…

- ❁ Cream-on-cream fabric for background 14in x 16in (35.5cm x 40.5cm)
- ❁ DMC stranded embroidery cotton (floss): ecru, black (310), old brick (355), light brick red (356), red brown (433), green (469), coral (758), brown (829), dark green ( 935) mauve (3041), lavender (3042), slate (3768), yellow (3820), caramel (3829)
- ❁ Fine-tipped fabric marking pen
- ❁ Buttons: seven small in assorted colours and two ladybirds (the bee buttons are optional)
- ❁ Iron-on stabilizer (optional)
- ❁ Light box (optional)
- ❁ Wooden picture frame with aperture at least 9in x 11in (22.9cm x 28cm)

**Finished size of stitchery:**
**7¾in x 9½in (19.7cm x 24.1cm)**

# Working the stitchery

**1** Begin by transferring the stitchery design using a light source such as a light box or a window, using the shapes provided in the Template section at the back of the book. Centre the background fabric right side up over the pattern and use a fine-tipped fabric marking pen to carefully trace all the stitchery lines. If you are using an iron-on stabilizer iron it on before starting the stitching. Place the shiny side of the stabilizer on to the wrong side of your fabric and follow the manufacturer's instructions to bond it in place.

**Tip**

Using an iron-on stabilizer on the back of your fabric will prevent shadows from the dark threads on the back of your work showing through on the front.

**2** Work the stitchery using the stitches and thread colours given opposite. Use two strands of embroidery thread unless otherwise stated. The stitches used are backstitch (BS), blanket stitch (BKS), chain stitch (CS), fly stitch (FS), French knot (FK), satin stitch (SS), stem stitch (STS) and running stitch (RS). Refer to Embroidery Stitches in Techniques for working the stitches. Numbers below correspond to DMC stranded embroidery thread codes.

**3** Once all the stitching has been completed frame your stitchery in a suitable frame. Alternatively, you could make the design up as a small wall hanging or cushion.

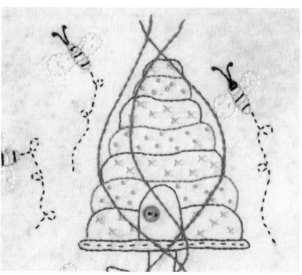

**Ecru**
Outline bees wings (BS)
Dots on wings (FK)

 **Black (310)**
Bee antennae (BS)
Dots on ends of antennae (FK)
Bees' trail (RS)
Bees' stripes, alternate (BS)

 **Old brick (355)**
Outline flowerpot (BS)
Right-hand delphinium flowers, every
third one from bottom (BKS)

 **Light brick red (356)**
Right-hand delphinium flowers, every
third one (BKS)
Cat's nose (SS)
Cat's mouth and inner ear (BS)

 **Red brown (433)**
Post and sign (BS)

 **Green (469)**
Dots in centre of delphinium (FKs)
Vine entwining beehive (STS)
Stems and leaves on delphiniums (BS)
Leaf veins on delphiniums (RS)

 **Coral (758)**
Right-hand delphinium flowers, every
third flower from top (BKS)

 **Brown (829)**
Beehive layers, alternating, starting from
bottom (BS)
Beehive door (BS)
Outline cat (BS)
Cat outline, left foot and eye outline (BS)
Cat's tummy (BKS)

 **Dark green (935)**
Leaves in flowerpot (BS)
Veins in leaves in flowerpot (FS)
Flower stems in pot (CS)

 **Mauve (3041)**
Left-hand delphinium flowers, alternating
from bottom (BKS)
Dots on writing (FK)

 **Lavender (3042)**
Left-hand delphinium flowers, alternating
from top (BKS)

 **Slate (3768)**
Flowers in flowerpot (BS)
Cat's eyes (FK)

 **Yellow (3820)**
Outline bees' bodies (BS)
Alternate stripes on bees' bodies (BS)
XXX on beehive (CS)
Dots on beehive (FK)

 **Caramel (3829)**
Outline ears, tail, right foot and stripes
on cat (BS)
Dashes inside stripes and tail of cat (RS)
Dots in delphinium centres, random (FK)
Beehive layers, alternating, starting from
second layer (BS)

# My Favourite Garden

Ｗhat could be more wonderful than a garden filled with all your favourite things – a cosy cottage, charming birdhouses and beehives, delicious citrus trees, pots crammed with colourful flowers and all alive with busy birds, butterflies and bees. This wall quilt has nine delightful scenes that combine appliqué with hand embroidery, reminding us what makes a garden a lovely place to be. A variety of attractive buttons are also used in the blocks, including a bird, butterfly, watering can, snail, bee and birdhouse. The blocks are framed by narrow strips of fabric in a Courthouse Steps pattern, with a simple border of pieced rectangles finishing off the design.

Two scenes from the quilt, reduced a little in size, are used again in two pretty pictures, set off nicely in circular frames. These would make a lovely housewarming present for a gardening friend.

# Garden Scenes Quilt

Soft, smudgy colours set off the garden-themed blocks nicely in this delightful quilt. Hand-painted buttons add dimension and texture. The buttons are available from some quilt shops or Lynette Anderson Designs – see Suppliers.

## You will need...

❀ Cream fabric for stitchery background ½yd (0.5m)

❀ Twelve coordinating prints for borders, a fat eighth of each, i.e., 9in x 21in (22.9cm x 53.3cm)

❀ Wadding (batting) 36in (91cm) square

❀ Backing fabric 36in (91cm) square

❀ Floral print for binding 7½in (19cm) (width of fabric)

❀ Hand-painted buttons: one each of birdhouse, watering can, daisy, snail, crow, ladybird, robin, bee and butterfly

❀ DMC stranded embroidery cotton (floss): dirty blue (413), soft green (642), dark brown (839), fawn (841), charcoal (844), soft blue (926) and dirty pink (3860)

❀ Fine-tipped fabric marking pen

❀ Iron-on stabilizer 18in (46cm) (optional)

❀ Light box (optional)

**Finished size:**
**31in (79cm) square**

## Preparing the background

**1** From the cream stitchery background fabric cut nine 5½in (14cm) squares (one square for each stitchery block). Take the twelve assorted coordinating prints and cut two 4½in x 3½in (11.4cm x 8.9cm) pieces for border rectangles and five 1in (2.5cm) strips (across fabric width) for the Courthouse Steps border around the blocks **(see Fig 1)**. From four assorted fabrics cut one 3½in (8.9cm) square, for the corner post squares in the outer border.

**Fig 1**

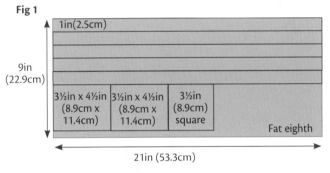

## Bordering the blocks

**2** Each block is bordered by a Courthouse Steps pattern. Take the 1in (2.5cm) strips you have cut and re-cut them to produce the following strips.

a – eighteen 1in x 5½in (2.5cm x 14cm)

b – eighteen 1in x 6½in (2.5cm x 16.5cm)

c – eighteen 1in x 6½in (2.5cm x 16.5cm)

d – eighteen 1in x 7½in (2.5cm x 19cm)

e – eighteen 1in x 7½in (2.5cm x 19cm)

f – eighteen 1in x 8½in (2.5cm x 21.6cm).

Using **Fig 2** as a guide and ¼in (6mm) seams, sew the strips to each centre square, pressing well. Each finished block should measure 8½in (21.6cm) square.

 **Tip** Remember when cutting the strips for the Courthouse Steps border that these are meant to look scrappy. To get this look I chose my fabrics individually for each block and cut them as they were required.

**Fig 2**

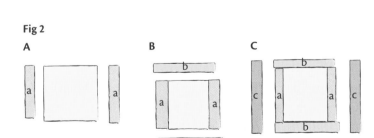

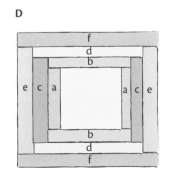

## Transferring the design

**3** Use the shapes provided in Templates (each block has its own templates). Using a light source such as a light box or window, position the centre of the block right side up over the pattern and use a fine-tipped fabric marking pen to carefully trace all the stitchery lines. If you are using an iron-on stitchery stabilizer iron it on before starting the stitching. Place the shiny side of the stabilizer on to the wrong side of your fabric and follow the manufacturer's instructions to bond it in place.

**Tip**
I like to use a fine (No.1) sepia (brown) fabric marking pen, as most thread colours will cover this colour easily.

## Working the appliqué

**4** Apply the shapes using the templates and your favourite method of appliqué. If you plan to use needle-turn appliqué you will need to add a ¼in (6mm) seam allowance to the shapes. If using fusible web appliqué you will need to reverse the shapes before using. I used needle-turn appliqué and made templates for the appliqué shapes from paper. See Working Appliqué in the Techniques section.

**5** Using the pictures throughout the project as a guide, position the appliqué shapes and glue baste or pin the shapes in place. I used a light box to help position the shapes and Roxanne's Glue Baste It, which has a nozzle that allows for fine placement of the glue.

## Working the stitchery

**6** Work the stitchery using the stitches and thread colours given with each block template. Use two strands of embroidery thread unless otherwise stated. The stitches used are backstitch (BS), blanket stitch (BKS), French knots (FK), lazy daisy (LD), running stitch (RS) and satin stitch (SS). Refer to Embroidery Stitches in Techniques for working the stitches. Numbers correspond to DMC stranded embroidery threads. Once the stitching on all of the blocks has been completed press your work.

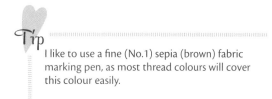

*Tip*

It is best to sew the buttons in place after the quilting has been finished – see step 9. Sew them on securely with matching thread.

## Joining the blocks

7 Lay all nine blocks out in order, or in an order of your choice. Using ¼in (6mm) seams join all the blocks together. First sew them into three rows of three and then join the rows together, as shown in **Fig 3A and B**. Press seams well.

**Fig 3**

**A**

| | | |
|---|---|---|
| Block 1 Birdhouse | Block 2 Cumquat tree | Block 3 Barrow |
| Block 4 Window box | Block 5 Crow cottage | Block 6 Herb pots |
| Block 7 Birdbath | Block 8 Beehive | Block 9 Butterfly Garden |

**B**

| | | |
|---|---|---|
| Block 1 Birdhouse | Block 2 Cumquat tree | Block 3 Barrow |
| Block 4 Window box | Block 5 Crow cottage | Block 6 Herb pots |
| Block 7 Birdbath | Block 8 Beehive | Block 9 Butterfly Garden |

−×−×−×−×−×−×−×−×−×−×−×−×−×

## Making the outer border

**8** Take the 3½in x 4½in (11.4 x 8.9cm) assorted print rectangles cut previously and arrange the fabrics in a pleasing way. You will need six rectangles for each side of the quilt (**Fig 4**). Once you are happy with the arrangement join the rectangles together with ¼in (6mm) seams. Now piece together another six rectangles, this time with a 3½in (11.4cm) square at each end. These strips are for the top and bottom borders. Attach these to the quilt and press the work.

**Fig 4**

**A**

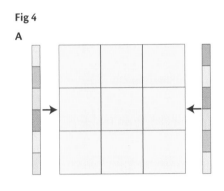

**B**

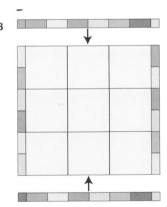

## Quilting

**9** The quilting uses threads that blend with the fabrics. Echo or contour quilt around each appliqué shape in the blocks. Quilt in the ditch of the seams in the Courthouse Steps border and the outer border. Quilt heart shapes in the outer border, within each fabric piece (the template is supplied in the Template section). Sew all the buttons into position when quilting is complete.

## Binding and finishing

**10** To bind the wall hanging cut a strip of binding fabric 1½in (3.8cm) wide x the necessary length (about 130in (330cm), on the straight grain. Press in ¼in (6mm) down the length. Bind the hanging following the instructions for Binding. Press and then label your quilt to finish, if desired – see Labelling Your Quilt.

# Flowerpot Pictures

Ideal for gift-giving, these sweet round frames are perfect for displaying the cute flowers in pots. Frames without glass were used to give a nice home-style feel to the finished items.

## You will need...

- ❀ Two pieces of cream fabric for stitchery background, each 6in (15.2cm) square
- ❀ Scraps of four assorted prints for the appliqué shapes
- ❀ DMC stranded embroidery cotton (floss): dirty blue (413), soft green (642), dark brown (839), fawn (841), charcoal (844), soft blue (926) and dirty pink (3860)
- ❀ Fine-tipped fabric marking pen in brown
- ❀ Two pieces of iron-on stabilizer, each 6in (15.2cm) square (optional)
- ❀ Light box (optional)
- ❀ Two picture frames to suit

**Finished design size:**
**3¼in (8.3cm) diameter (excluding frame)**

## Transferring the design

**1** Use the shapes provided in Templates at the back of the book. Using a light source such as a light box or window, position the centre of the block right side up over the pattern and use a fine-tipped fabric marking pen to carefully trace all the stitchery lines. If using an iron-on stitchery stabilizer iron it on before starting the stitching. Place the shiny side of the stabilizer on to the wrong side of the fabric and follow the manufacturer's instructions to bond it in place.

## Working the appliqué

**2** Apply the shapes using the templates and your favourite method of appliqué. If using needle-turn appliqué add ¼in (6mm) seam allowance to the shapes. If using fusible web appliqué, reverse the shapes before using. I used needle-turn appliqué and made templates for the appliqué shapes from paper. See Working Appliqué in the Techniques section.

**3** Using the pictures as a guide, position the appliqué shapes and then glue baste or pin the shapes in place. I used a light box to help position the shapes and Roxanne's Glue Baste It, which has a nozzle that allows for fine placement of the glue. Stitch the appliqué shapes in position using a blind hem stitch. I used thread matching my background fabric so it didn't show.

## Working the stitchery

**4** Work the stitchery using the stitches and thread colours given with each template. Use two strands of embroidery thread unless otherwise stated. The stitches used are backstitch (BS), cross stitch (CS), French knots (FK), lazy daisy (LD), running stitch (RS) and satin stitch (SS). Refer to Embroidery Stitches in Techniques for working the stitches. Numbers correspond to DMC stranded embroidery threads.

**Tip**

If you like to work your embroidery in a hoop or frame, allow a little more fabric for mounting in the hoop. This can be trimmed down later.

**5** When all the stitching has been completed press your work and frame your stitcheries as desired.

# Go Wild Garden

*I*f you have your own garden it's your place to go wild in and do what pleases you. For this stunning quilt I chose a traditional block called Busy Bee, which is really easy to make, and had fun adding some garden-themed appliqué shapes to enlarge the block size. The repetitive 18in (45.7cm) block allows you to make the quilt larger or smaller. The appliqué is easily created with fusible web, with a lovely blanket stitch edging in black thread. A dark green border frames the blocks, while an outer border made of squares of the same fabrics used in the blocks ties the whole design together.

A plump cushion finishes off this chapter and is a great way to practise the techniques used in the quilt as it uses just one block. The colours are the same warm, earthy tones with a touch of blue for contrast.

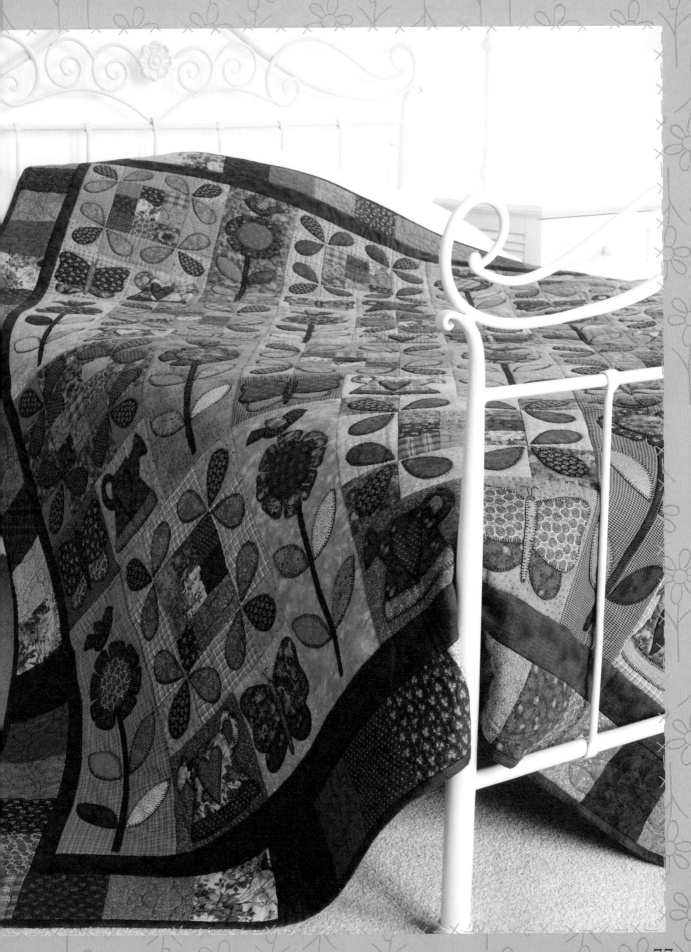

# Go Wild Quilt

I love the muted colours in this quilt and privately call it my muddy garden quilt, because as a child I can remember playing outside in the mud while mum weeded the garden. Fabrics cut as fat quarters and fat eighths are used for this quilt. A fat quarter is approximately 18in x 22in (45.7cm x 55.9cm) and a fat eighth is 9in x 22in (22.9cm x 56cm).

## You will need...

* Background fabrics, twelve different fat quarters
* Green fabrics, five different fat quarters
* Blue fabrics, five different fat quarters
* Burgundy fabrics, five different fat quarters
* Black print for bees' bodies, one fat quarter
* Black print for birds' bodies, one fat eighth
* Dark green fabric for inner border, stems and leaves ¾yd (0.75m)
* Fusible web (such as Bondaweb/ Vliesofix) 3yd (3.25m)
* Backing fabric 70in x 90in (178cm x 228cm)
* Wadding (batting) 70in x 90in (178cm x 228cm)
* Fabric for binding ½yd (0.5m)
* Black stranded cotton (floss)
* Sewing and quilting threads
* Appliqué mat (optional)

**Finished size:**
63in x 83in (160cm x 211cm)

## Cutting the fabrics

**1** From each background fat quarter cut the following pieces **(see Fig 1)**.

Four rectangles 3½in x 6½in (8.9cm x 16.5cm) for the Busy Bee blocks.

Four 3½in (8.9cm) squares for the Busy Bee blocks.

Two 6½in (16.5cm) squares for the butterfly/watering can background.

One rectangle 6½in x 18½in (16.5cm x 47cm) for the sunflower background. The remaining fabric will be used for appliqué later.

From each of the print fabrics (five green, five burgundy and five blue) cut the following **(Fig 2)**.

Eight 2½in (6.3cm) squares for the nine-patch centres of the Busy Bee blocks.

Five 4½in (11.4cm) squares for the outer border. The remaining fabric will be used for appliqué later.

From dark green border fabric cut three 2½in (6.3cm) wide strips across the width of the fabric and four 1½in (3.8cm) strips. Place these strips aside for later. The remaining fabric will be used for the sunflower stems and some leaves.

## Making the Busy Bee blocks

**2** You will need to make twelve of these blocks. Starting with the nine-patch centres, first take the 2½in (6.3cm) squares cut previously (120 in total, that is, eight from each of the fifteen prints, although you will only use 108 of these). With random colour placement and using ¼in (6mm) seams join the squares to form three rows of three **(see Fig 3)**. Join the rows together to form the nine-patch.

**Fig 1**

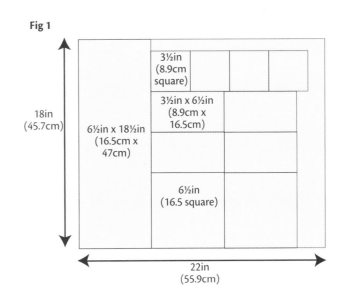

**Fig 2**

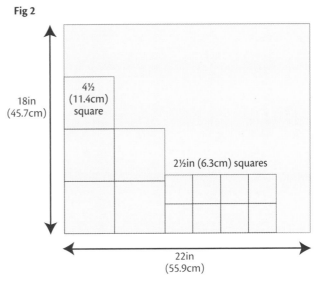

**Fig 3**

A    B    C

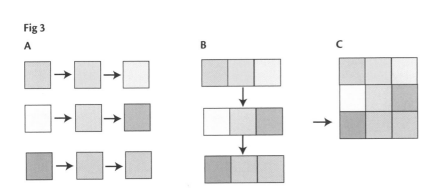

3 Take the 3½in (8.9cm) squares and the 3½in x 6½in (8.9cm x 16.5cm)
rectangles cut previously from the background fabrics. Join a rectangle
to the top and bottom of each nine-patch **(Fig 4)**. Now join a 3½in (8.9cm)
corner square to each end of a 3½in x 6½in (8.9cm x 16.5cm) rectangle and
join this unit to one side of the nine-patch block. Repeat for the other side.

**Fig 4**

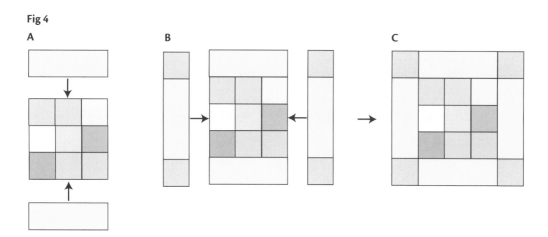

A          B          C

## Making the background blocks

4 The Busy Bee blocks now need to be joined to
the fabric pieces that will make up the appliqué
backgrounds, using ¼in (6mm) seams. **Fig 5** shows
the arrangement of the pieces but note that six of the
blocks are made in one arrangement, Block A, and six
are reversed for Block B – see pictures below.

## Working the appliqué

5 When the blocks are made, start the appliqué,
using the shapes provided in Templates. A fusible
web method was used, so reverse the shapes using a
light source such as a light box or window. Follow the
instructions for the Fusible Web Method. You could
use an appliqué mat.

**Fig 5**

Busy Bee block 12½in
(31.7cm) square

18½in
x 6½in
(47cm x
16.5cm)

6½in
(16.5cm)
square

6½in
(16.5cm)
square

**Block A – make 6**

**Block B – make 6**

*Tip*

An appliqué mat is useful because you can iron some of the underneath appliqué pieces in place, thus stopping them moving out of position. You can remove and re-position fabrics fused to an appliqué mat, but not fabrics already fused to fabrics.

6 When the appliqués are fused into position use two strands of black embroidery thread to blanket stitch around the edges of the shapes.

## Joining the blocks

7 Now join the blocks together. Join two rows of three blocks with the sunflower block on the left and two rows of three blocks with the sunflower block on the right. Then, alternating the two rows, join them together to form four rows of three **(Fig 6)**.

## Adding the inner border

8 Take the dark green border strips previously cut and join the 2½in (6.3cm) strips to make two long strips each 2½in x 54½in (6.3cm x 138.4cm) – these are for the top and bottom borders. Check your quilt measurement first as it may differ from mine. Join these borders to the quilt (see Adding a Border in the Techniques section). Now join the narrower 1½in (3.8cm) strips to make two long strips each 1½in x 75½in (3.8cm x 192cm) – these are for the two side borders. Join these to the sides of the quilt.

**Fig 6**

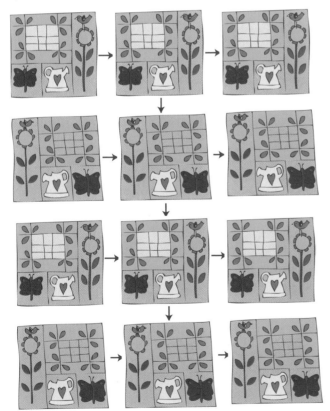

## Adding the pieced border

9 Take the 4½in (11.4cm) squares cut from the appliqué fabrics earlier and using a ¼in (6mm) seam allowance join them to form two rows of fourteen squares and then two rows of twenty-one squares – these will be the top and bottom borders and the two side borders respectively **(Fig 7)**. Join the top and bottom borders to the quilt top first and press the seams. Now add the two side borders and press the seams.

## Quilting

10 Your quilt top is now ready for quilting, so quilt using your preferred method. Echo or contour quilt around each appliqué shape in all of the blocks. Quilt in the ditch of the seams of the blocks. Quilt a sunflower and leaf motif in the outer border, repeating around the border as necessary – a template is supplied in the Template section.

**Fig 7**

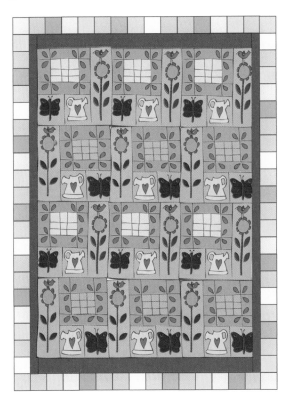

## Binding and finishing

11 To bind the quilt cut a strip 1½in (3.8cm) wide x the necessary length (about 300in/ 762cm), cut on the straight grain. Press in ¼in (6mm) down the length of the strip. Bind the quilt following the instructions for Binding in the Techniques section. Press the finished binding and then label your quilt to finish, if desired – see Labelling Your Quilt.

# Garden Pillow

Bring the garden indoors with this lovely patchwork and appliqué pillow.
One Busy Bee block combined with some blanket stitch appliqué units
makes this a great project for a beginner.

## You will need...

❃ Tan fabric for background 7¾in (20cm)
   (width of fabric)

❃ Cream-on-cream fabric for background
   7in (17.8cm) square

❃ Tan check for background 6½in
   (16.5cm) square

❃ Three assorted blue prints 6in (15.2cm)
   square of each

❃ Three assorted red prints 6in (15.2cm)
   square of each

❃ Three assorted burgundy prints 6in
   (15.2cm) square of each

❃ Blue floral print for pillow back 20in
   (50.8cm) square

❃ DMC stranded embroidery cotton
   (floss): red (816), soft blue (932) and
   burgundy (3802)

❃ Calico 20in (50.8cm) square

❃ Wadding (batting) 20in (50.8cm)
   square

❃ Blue floral fabric for binding 3in
   (7.6cm) (width of fabric)

❃ Zip 15¾in (40cm) long

❃ Pillow pad 18in (46cm) square

**Finished size:**
**18in (46cm) square**

## Cutting the fabrics

**1** From the tan background fabric cut one piece 6½in x 18½in (16.5cm x 47cm), four pieces 3½in x 6½in (8.9cm x 16.5cm) and one 6½in (16.5cm) square. From the tan check background fabric cut one 6½in (16.5cm) square.

From the cream fabric cut four 3½in (8.9cm) squares. From assorted print fabrics cut a total of nine 2½in (6.4cm) squares.

## Making the Busy Bee block

**2** Assemble the nine-patch block from the nine 2½in (8.9cm) squares. With random colour placement and using ¼in (6mm) seams join the squares to form three rows of three **(see Fig 1)**. Join the three rows together to form the nine-patch.

**3** Take two of the 3½in x 6½in (8.9cm x 16.5cm) pieces and join them to the top and bottom of the nine-patch unit. Now join a 3½in (8.9cm) cream square to each end of a 3½in x 6½in (8.9cm x 16.5cm) rectangle and join this unit to one side of the nine-patch block. Repeat for the other side, to make the arrangement shown in **Fig 2**.

**Fig 1**

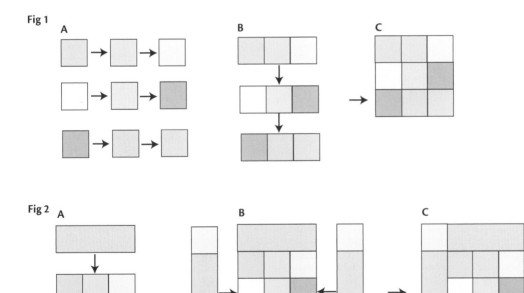

**Fig 2**

## Making the background blocks

4 The Busy Bee block now needs to be joined to the fabric pieces that will make up the appliqué backgrounds, using ¼in (6mm) seams. **Fig 3** shows the arrangement of the pieces.

**Fig 3**

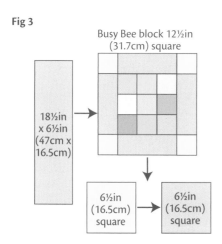

Busy Bee block 12½in (31.7cm) square

18½in x 6½in (47cm x 16.5cm)

6½in (16.5cm) square

6½in (16.5cm) square

## Working the appliqué

5 Once all the blocks have been joined you can work the appliqué. Use the shapes provided in Templates at the back of the book. Fusible web was used to do the appliqué, so you will need to reverse the shapes using a light source such as a light box or a window. Follow the instructions in the Fusible Web Method in the Techniques section. If you are using an appliqué mat see also the instructions for the Appliqué Mat Method.

6 When the appliqués are fused into position use two strands of embroidery thread to work blanket stitch around the edges of the shapes, matching the red, soft blue and burgundy thread colours to the fabrics.

## Quilting

7 I hand quilted my pillow front, layering the front with wadding (batting) and calico and quilting around each appliqué shape. A simple criss-cross pattern was quilted in the nine-patch block.

## Inserting the zip and making up

8 From the pillow backing fabric cut two pieces 18½in x 9¾in (47cm x 24.8cm). Press ½in (1.3cm) to the wrong side of the fabric along one long side of each piece (Fig 4).

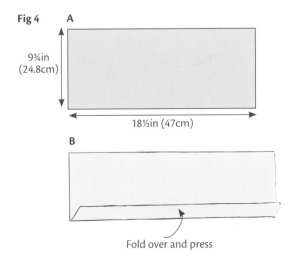

Fig 4

A

9¾in
(24.8cm)

18½in (47cm)

B

Fold over and press

9 Place the zip in position on one side and pin in place. Using the zip foot on your machine, stitch the first side of the zip into place (Fig 5). Position and pin the other side of the zip and stitch in place.

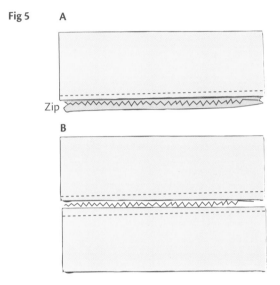

Fig 5  A

Zip

B

10 Take the back and the front of the pillow, place them wrong sides together (right sides out) on a flat surface and pin them together. Sew the pieces together all around the edge, using a ¼in (6mm) seam.

## Binding

11 To bind the pillow cut a strip 1½in (3.8cm) wide x the necessary length (about 80in/ 203cm), cut on the straight grain. Press in ¼in (6mm) down the length of the strip. Bind the pillow following the instructions for Binding in the Techniques section. Press the binding and then insert the pillow pad inside the cover to finish.

# Materials and Equipment

*T*he projects each have a list of the materials and equipment required and the basics are described here, but there's no reason why you can't experiment, especially with fabrics and embellishments.

## Fabrics and wadding (batting)

For many people 100% cotton fabrics are the ones of choice for patchwork and quilting but sometimes it's great to try other types of fabrics. The fabrics used to back quilts, bind quilts or to line projects such as bags can really be anything you like but cotton is the easiest to handle.

Quilt wadding (batting) is rated by its weight and is sold in standard sizes and by the yard or metre. It is available in polyester, cotton, wool and various blends and for hand and machine quilting. Thinner wadding tends to be used when machine quilting. I prefer to use Matilda's Own wool/poly blend, which is pre-washed, pre-shrunk, fully machine washable and comes in white and charcoal.

## Threads

Many people like to use 100% cotton thread for machine piecing and machine quilting. Polyester mixes are also popular. Threads for hand quilting can be almost anything you like. If you want the quilting to blend or tone with the fabrics then use a cotton or polyester.

For my stitcheries I mostly use DMC stranded cottons. These embroidery threads are in six-stranded skeins that can be split into separate strands and are available the world over in a very wide range of colours. I also use some Cosmo threads, which you may be able to source.

## Fusible web and interfacing

Fusible web is also referred to as iron-on adhesive and is an ultra-thin sheet of adhesive backed with a special paper. When the web is placed between two fabrics, the heat of an iron causes the glue to melt and fuse the fabrics together – perfect for appliqué (see Fusible Web Method). There are various makes of fusible web, including Bondaweb (Vliesofix or Wonder Under) and Steam-A-Seam2. Read the manufacturer's instructions before use.

Fusible interfacing works on the same principle but is single-sided. It is used to stiffen and strengthen fabrics. An iron-on stabilizer can also be used to strengthen a fabric, making it more able to support embroidery stitches. It needs to be ironed on before the stitching is started.

## Buttons

I like to use buttons in my work, not just functional ones but also to represent animals' eyes, flower centres and so on. I have my own range of really cute buttons in all sorts of shapes – see Suppliers.

## Glues

There are temporary glues available that are very useful, especially for appliqué. I find Roxanne's Glue Baste-It ™ excellent as it has a fine nozzle for accurate placement of the glue. It is only a temporary glue but is handy for holding pieces in place instead of using pins. You will also need a fast-tack craft glue for fixing the Gardener's Scissor Keeper together. Always follow the instructions on the glue packet and use in a well-ventilated room.

## Equipment

There are many tools and gadgets you could buy for patchwork and quilting but a basic tool kit is all you really need to start with.

### Basic tool kit

- ❋ Quilter's ruler
- ❋ Rotary cutter and mat
- ❋ Scissors
- ❋ Tape measure
- ❋ Needles
- ❋ Pins and safety pins
- ❋ Thimble
- ❋ Template plastic
- ❋ Marking pen
- ❋ Iron
- ❋ Sewing machine
- ❋ Embroidery hoop
- ❋ Fabric glue

## Rotary cutter, ruler and mat

Patchwork is easier and quicker with a rotary cutter, ruler and mat, especially for quilt making. You will find a self-healing cutting mat 18in x 24in is very useful and a 45mm or 60mm diameter rotary cutter.

## Pins and needles

You will need pins for piecing patchwork and for fastening the layers of a quilt together. Safety pins could also be used for securing the quilt sandwich. Alternatively, spray adhesives are available for this.

You will need a selection of hand sewing needles for embroidery and quilting and machine needles for piecing and quilting. I use Clover No. 9 embroidery needles and love the smooth, quality finish the needles have. Their gold eye makes them easy to thread.

## Marking pens

In this book markers are mostly used to mark stitchery designs on to fabric. I use a fine Zig Millenium or Pigma Micron permanent marker pen, usually in brown. There are also water- and air-soluble pens that can be used to mark fabric temporarily.

## Template plastic

This is a transparent plastic that can be used to create templates which can be used many times. It is available from craft shops and patchwork and quilting suppliers. The template is traced on to the plastic and cut out with sharp scissors (don't use your fabric scissors!). Use a permanent marker to label the template.

## Masking tape

This is very useful to mark straight quilting lines and is used in several of the projects. Simply place a long strip of the tape where you want to quilt and sew along the edge of the tape. A low-tack tape is easy to remove and doesn't leave any marks.

## Appliqué mat

An appliqué mat is a large non-stick sheet, usually made from Teflon. One advantage to using an appliqué mat is that you can iron some of the underneath pieces in place, thus stopping them moving out of position, which allows you to position the top layers with ease.

You can remove and re-position fabrics fused to an appliqué mat, but not fabrics already fused to fabrics. Keep your mat rolled when not in use and it will last for years.

## Light box

This is a useful piece of equipment for tracing designs but can be expensive so try using a well-lit window instead. Tape the design to the light box (or window), tape the fabric on top and trace the design on to the fabric. I also use a light under a glass table, which works well and stops my arms getting tired when standing at a window!

# Techniques

This section describes the basic techniques you will need to make and finish off the projects in this book, from transferring designs to binding a finished quilt. Beginners in particular should find it very useful.

## Sewing seams

Patchwork or pieced work does require that your seams are accurate in order that your blocks will fit together nicely. Maintaining an accurate ¼in (6mm) seam allowance where stated will give the best results. For really accurate piecing sew a *bare* ¼in (6mm) seam, as this will allow for the thickness of thread and the tiny amount of fabric taken up when the seam is pressed.

## Pressing work

Your work will look its best if you press it well. Generally, seams are pressed towards the darker fabric to avoid darker colours showing through on the right side. If joining seams are pressed in opposite directions they will lock together nicely and create the flattest join. Press (don't iron) and be very careful with steam, as this can stretch fabric, particularly edges cut on the bias.

## Using templates

The project templates are given after this section and most will need to be enlarged to full size – please read all of the instructions with each template carefully. Once a template is the size required you can trace it on to paper or thin card, cut it out and use it as a pattern to cut the shape from paper. Before cutting out check whether a ¼in (6mm) seam allowance is needed. If using a template for needle-turn appliqué a seam allowance will be required, but will not be needed if you are using a fusible web appliqué technique.

## Reversing templates

Sometimes it is necessary to reverse a template, so that a design will appear facing the other way and templates used for fusible web appliqué will need to be reversed. One way to do this is to photocopy it and place the copy on to a light source with the template face down rather than right side up. The design is then reversed and you can trace it as normal. You could also trace the template on to tracing paper, turn the tracing paper over and trace the template again on to paper.

## Transferring designs

Designs can be transferred on to fabric in various ways. I use a light source, such as a light box, a window or a light under a glass table. Iron your fabric so it is free of creases. Place the design right side up and then the fabric right side up on top, taping in place if necessary. Use a fine-tipped fabric marking pen or a pencil to trace the design. If the marks might show later use a temporary marker, such as an air-erasable or water-soluble one.

# Working appliqué

Appliqué is the technique of fixing one fabric shape on top of another. I have used two methods – needle-turn appliqué and fusible web appliqué. You may also like to use an appliqué mat.

## Needle-turn method

This is a traditional method of hand appliqué where each appliqué piece has a seam turned under all round and is stitched into position on the background fabric. The appliqué shapes may be drawn freehand or templates used.

1 Mark around the template on the wrong side of your fabric and then mark another line further out all round for the seam allowance. This is usually ¼in (6mm) but depends on the size of the appliqué piece being stitched and type of fabric being used. Smaller pieces may only need a ⅛in (3mm) allowance. Clip into the seam allowance on concave curves (the inward ones) to make it easier to turn the seam under.

2 For each appliqué piece turn the seam allowance under all round and press. Position the appliqué on the background fabric and stitch into place with tiny slip stitches. Press when finished. Some people use the needle to turn the seam under as they stitch the appliqué in place.

## Fusible web method

Fusible web has an adhesive that melts with the heat of a medium-hot iron, so when the web is placed between two fabrics the heat causes the fabrics to fuse together.

1 When using templates for fusible web appliqué they need to be flipped or reversed because you will be drawing the shape on the back of the fabric – see Reversing Templates.

2 Trace around each template on to the paper side of the fusible web, leaving about ½in (1.3cm) around each shape. Cut out roughly around each shape. Iron the fusible web, paper side up, on to the wrong side of the appliqué fabric. Cut out accurately on your drawn line.

3 When the web is cool, peel off the backing paper and place the appliqué in position on your project, right side up. (Check the template to see which pieces need to go under other pieces, shown by dotted lines on the patterns.) Fuse into place with a medium-hot iron for about ten seconds. Allow to cool.

4 The edge of the appliqué can be secured further by stitches. I normally use blanket stitch as I like the hand-crafted look but machine satin stitch can also be used.

## Appliqué mat method

Using your ironing board as a work area, place your appliqué mat over the template. Remove the backing paper from each appliqué piece as required and position on the mat. Some pieces need to go beneath other pieces and these are shown by dotted lines on the template. When satisfied with the positions, iron into place. Once cool, peel the shape from the mat, place on the background fabric and fuse with the iron.

## English Paper Piecing

This type of patchwork is also called English patchwork and uses templates, usually made of paper or thin card, which fabric pieces are wrapped around and tacked (basted) to. The patches are hand sewn together and the papers then removed.

1 From a master template, create enough paper templates for the project. When cutting out the fabric pieces allow for a ¼in (6mm) seam all round.

2 Follow **Fig 1A–E** and pin a paper template to a fabric shape. Fold the seam allowance over the edges of the template, tacking (basting) in place through all layers. Alternatively, use a fabric glue pen. Keep the fabric firm around the paper shape and tuck in all points neatly. Repeat with all the fabric pieces.

3 Place two fabric shapes right sides together, aligning edges and use small whip stitches to sew them together through the folded fabric but *not* through the paper. Place a third fabric shape right sides together with the second and sew together. Continue building the design in this way. Once all stitching is finished remove the tacking and the papers.

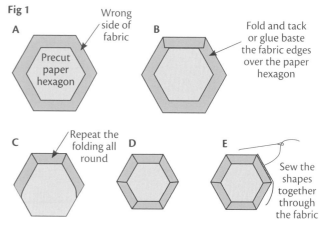

Fig 1

A — Precut paper hexagon — Wrong side of fabric

B — Fold and tack or glue baste the fabric edges over the paper hexagon

C — Repeat the folding all round

D

E — Sew the shapes together through the fabric

## Making yoyos

Yoyos are sometimes called Suffolk puffs and add a lovely three-dimensional look to patchwork.

1 Using a fine-tipped pencil or fabric marking pen, draw around a circular template on the wrong side of your fabrics. Cut out on the line (the seam allowance is included in project templates).

2 Thread your needle with a double strand of sewing cotton and knot one end. Take one of the circles and with the wrong side facing you fold over approximately ¼in (6mm). Make a running stitch around the entire edge (**see Fig 2A**), turning the ¼in (6mm) in as you go and gathering it slightly.

3 Once you are back to where you started, gently pull on the thread to gather it. Wriggle the yoyo between your fingers to get it into shape (**Fig 2B**). Pull the thread firmly once you are happy with the look and tie the thread off at the back.

**Fig 2**

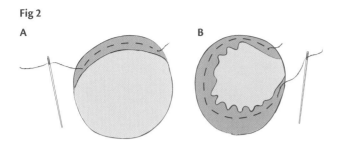

2 Measure the quilt height through the centre, including the top and bottom borders you have just added **(Fig 3B)**. Cut the side borders to this measurement, sew them in place and press. To add a second border, repeat steps 1 and 2.

**Fig 3**

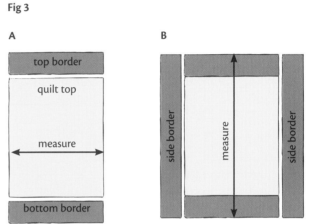

## Adding a border

A border frames a quilt and can tie the whole design together. Borders can be plain and simple or pieced and I have used both types in this book. Most are sewn on with straight or butted corners.

1 Calculate what length the border should be by measuring the width of the quilt through the centre and cut the top and bottom borders to this measurement **(Fig 3A)**. Measuring this way is more accurate than measuring at the ends, which may have spread a little during the making of the quilt. Sew the top and bottom borders to the quilt top using ¼in (6mm) seams and then press.

## Joining Strips

Sometimes you will need to join fabric strips together to make them long enough for borders or binding. Joining them with a diagonal seam at a 45 degree angle will make them less noticeable, as will pressing the seam open **(Fig 4)**.

**Fig 4**

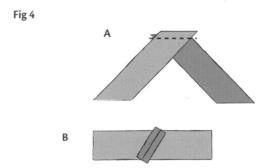

# Making a Quilt Sandwich

A quilt sandwich is a term used to describe the three layers of a quilt – the top, the wadding (batting) and the backing. These layers need to be secured together so that a quilt will hang correctly and be free of puckers. Any hand or machine quilting you plan to do will look much better if the layers are secured well.

1 Press your backing fabric and hang out your wadding if necessary to reduce creases. Cut out your wadding and backing about 4in (10.2cm) larger all round than the quilt top. Prepare the top by cutting off or tying in stray ends, pressing it and sorting out seam allowances so they lay as flat as possible.

2 Lay the backing fabric right side down on a smooth surface and tape the corners to keep it flat. Put the wadding (batting) on top, smoothing out wrinkles. Now put the quilt top right side up on top.

3 Securing the three layers together can be done in various ways. Some people use pins or safety pins, some use tacking (basting), others use a spray glue. If using pins or tacking, use a grid pattern, spacing the lines out about 3–6in (7.6–15.2cm) apart. Tack the outside edges of the quilt sandwich too, about ½in (1.3cm) in from the edge. The sandwich is now ready for quilting.

## Quilting

Quilting not only adds texture and interest to a quilt but also secures all the layers together. I have used a combination of hand and machine quilting on the projects in this book. The hand quilting stitch is really just a running stitch and ideally the length of the stitches and the spaces in between need to be small and even. Machine quilting has a more continuous look and the stitch length is usually about 10–12 stitches per 1in (2.5cm) and may depend on the fabric and threads you are using. How much or how little quilting you do is up to you but aim for a fairly even amount over the whole quilt. When starting and finishing hand or machine quilting, the starting knot and the thread end need to be hidden in the wadding (batting).

I have described within the projects where I quilted the projects in this book. Some areas you might consider quilting are as follows.
• Quilt in the ditch (that is in the seams between the blocks or the units that make up the blocks).
• Echo or contour quilt around motifs, about ¼in (6mm) out from the edge of the shape.
• Background quilt in a grid or hatched pattern of regularly spaced lines.
• Motif or pattern quilt within blocks or borders by selecting a specific motif, such as a heart or flower.

## Marking a Quilt

If you need to mark a quilting design on your top this can be done before or after you have made the quilt sandwich – most people do it before. There are many marking pens and pencils available but test them on scrap fabric first. If you are machine quilting, marking lines are more easily covered up. For hand quilting you might prefer to use a removable marker or a light pencil. Some water-erasable markers are set by the heat of an iron so take care when pressing.

# Binding

Binding a quilt creates a neat and secure edge all round. Binding may be single or double, with double binding being more durable and probably best for bed quilts.

1 Measure your quilt top around all edges and add about 8in (20.3cm) extra – this is the length of binding you need. Cut 2½in (6.3cm) wide strips and join them all together to make the length needed. Fold the binding in half along the length and press.

2 Start midway along one side of the quilt and pin the binding along the edge, aligning raw edges. Start stitching about 6in (15.2cm) away from the end of the binding and stitch through all layers using a ¼in (6mm) seam. When you reach a corner stop ¼in (6mm) away from the end (see Fig 5A).

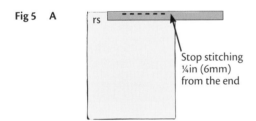

**Fig 5**   **A**

Stop stitching
¼in (6mm)
from the end

3 Remove the work from the machine and fold the binding up, northwards, so it is aligned straight with the edge of the quilt (Fig 5B).

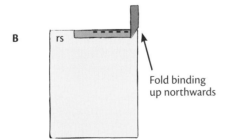

**B**

Fold binding
up northwards

4 Hold the corner and fold the binding back down, southwards, aligning it with the raw edge and with the folded corner square. Pin in position and then begin sewing again, from the top and over the fold, continuing down the next edge (Fig 5C). Repeat with the other corners.

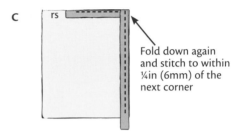

**C**

Fold down again
and stitch to within
¼in (6mm) of the
next corner

5 When you are nearing the starting point stop 6in (15.2cm) away. Fold back the beginning and end of the binding, so they touch and mark these folds with a pin. Cut the binding ¼in (6mm) from the pin, open out the binding and join with a ¼in (6mm) seam. Press the seam open, re-fold it and slipstitch in place.

6 Fold the binding over to the back of the quilt and slipstitch it in place all round. Fold the mitres at the corners neatly and secure with tiny slipstitches.

# Labelling your Quilt

When you have finished your quilt it is important to label it, even if the information you put on the label is just your name and the date. When looking at antique quilts it is always interesting to piece together information about the quilt, so you can be sure that any extra information you put on your label will be of immense interest to quilters of the future. A very simple method of labelling is to write on a piece of calico with a permanent marker pen and then appliqué this to the back of your quilt.

# Embroidery stitches

I have used various stitches to create the stitcheries on the projects in this book.

They are all easy to work and fun to do. Follow these simple diagrams.

## Blanket stitch

Blanket stitch is a useful stitch. It can be used to edge appliqué motifs and be stitched in a circle for flowers such as hollyhocks. This is my version of this stitch. The conventional method often allows the thread to slip under the edges of the appliqué, allowing raw edges to be seen and this method avoids that.

Start at the edge of the appliqué shape, taking the needle through to the back of the work and come back through to the front of the shape that you are appliquéing, a small distance in from the edge where you started. Pull the thread through to form a loop. Put your needle through the loop from front to back, making sure the loop is not twisted. As you pull the thread into place lift the stitch slightly so that it sits on top of the raw edge rather than sliding underneath. Pull the thread firmly into place to avoid loose, floppy stitches. Continue on to make the next stitch.

## Backstitch

Backstitch is an outlining stitch that I also use to 'draw' parts of a design. It is really easy to work and can follow any parts of a design you choose.

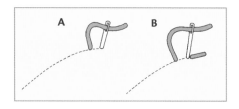

## Chain stitch

This stitch can be worked in straight or curved lines and as a detached stitch. I've used it as flower stems.

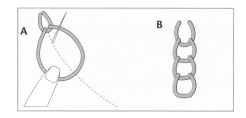

## Cross stitch

A simple cross stitch is used in many of the stitcheries to add pattern, particularly on animal coats.

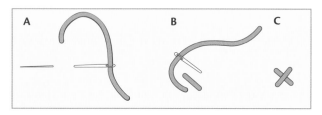

## Fly stitch

This stitch has been used as a single stitch for leaf detailing. The final part of the stitch can be longer if desired.

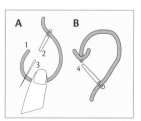

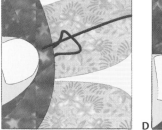
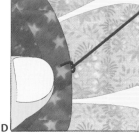
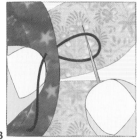

# Detached chain stitch

Detached chain stitch can be worked in lines and curves or more densely side by side to fill areas of a design. I've used it on some of the flowers.

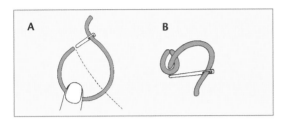

# French knot

These little knots are easy to form and are useful for eyes and other details.

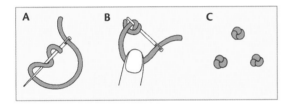

# Herringbone stitch

This stitch can be used to outline areas or form patterns. It was used to stitch the Gardener's Scissor Keeper together.

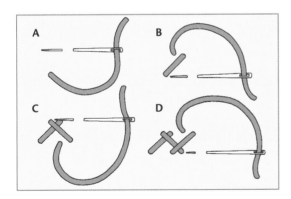

# Long stitch

Long stitch is just that, a single long stitch. It is useful for coat markings, cat's whiskers and so on.

# Lazy daisy stitch

This decorative stitch is great for flowers especially if the stitches are worked in a circle.

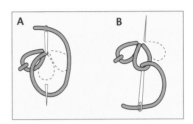

# Long and short stitch

This stitch combines a short stitch and a long stitch in an alternating pattern that locks together to create a densely worked area.

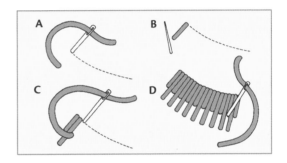

# Running stitch

These are evenly spaced stitches that can run in any direction or pattern you choose. Quilting stitch is a running stitch.

# Satin stitch

This stitch is used to fill in areas of a design, with long stitches worked smoothly side by side.

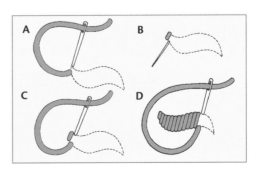

# Templates

This section contains the stitchery and appliqué templates for the projects. Most templates have had to be reduced to fit the page so please read the instructions with each template carefully. Some templates will need to have seam allowances added and this is marked on the template. See also Using Templates, Reversing Templates and Transferring Designs.

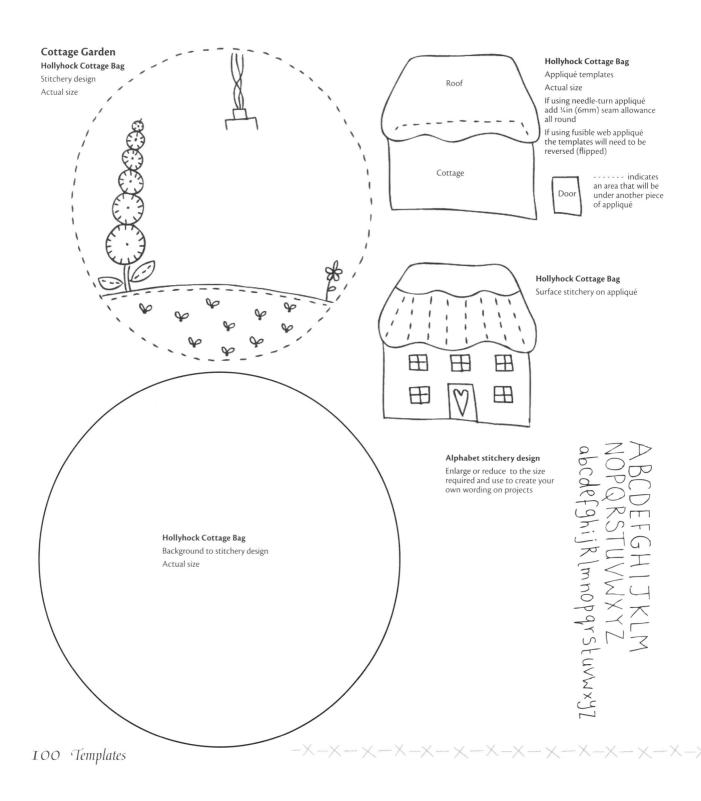

**Cottage Garden**
**Hollyhock Cottage Bag**
Stitchery design
Actual size

**Hollyhock Cottage Bag**
Appliqué templates
Actual size

If using needle-turn appliqué add ¼in (6mm) seam allowance all round

If using fusible web appliqué the templates will need to be reversed (flipped)

- - - - - indicates an area that will be under another piece of appliqué

Roof

Cottage

Door

**Hollyhock Cottage Bag**
Surface stitchery on appliqué

**Hollyhock Cottage Bag**
Background to stitchery design
Actual size

**Alphabet stitchery design**
Enlarge or reduce to the size required and use to create your own wording on projects

ABCDEFGHIJKLM
NOPQRSTUVWXYZ
abcdefghijklmnopqrstuvwxyz

**Hollyhock Needle Case**
Actual size

a b c d e f g h i j k l m n o p q r s
t u v w x y z

**Hollyhock Needle Case**
Stitchery design for inside case
Actual size

You could stitch your name here or create your own wording using the alphabet provided

Heart

**Hollyhock Needle Case**

Applique heart template for inside case

Actual size

**Gardener's Scissor Keeper**
Stitchery design
Actual size

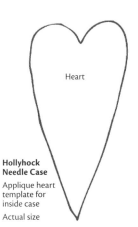

**Gardener's Scissor Keeper**
Actual size

**Scissor Keeper - back**
Cut the following:
2 from thin card
1 from thin wadding
1 from template plastic
1 from dark brown floral print (add seam allowance)
1 from dark brown floral print (add seam allowance)

**Scissor Keeper - front**
Cut the following:
2 from thin card
1 from thin wadding
1 from template plastic
1 from dark brown floral print (add seam allowance)
1 from dark brown floral print (add seam allowance

## Vintage Flowers

**Flower Spool Quilt**
Appliqué templates
Actual size

If using needle-turn appliqué add ¼in (6mm) seam allowance all round
If using fusible web appliqué the templates will need to be reversed (flipped)

- - - - - - - indicates an area that will be under another piece of appliqué

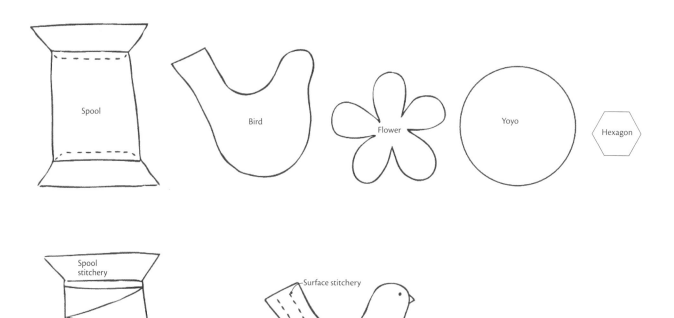

## Birdhouse Garden

**Birdhouse Bag**

Appliqué templates

Actual size

If using needle-turn appliqué add ¼in (6mm) seam allowance all round.

If using fusible web appliqué the templates will need to be reversed

- - - - - indicates an area that will be under another piece of appliqué

**Little Bird Purse**

Appliqué templates

Actual size

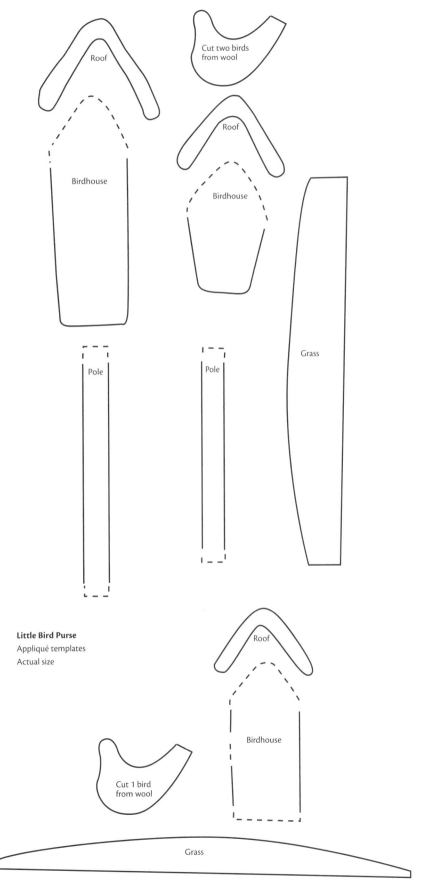

## Birdhouse Garden
**Birdhouse Bag**
Stitchery design
Actual size

Red lines indicate appliqué placement
Black lines indicate stitchery lines
Blue lines indicate surface stitchery on appliqué

 Flower for button

**Little Bird Purse**
Stitchery design
Actual size

Red lines indicate appliqué placement
Black lines indicate stitchery lines
Blue lines indicate surface stitchery on appliqué

**Birdhouse Garden**

**Birdhouse Bag**

Patchwork templates

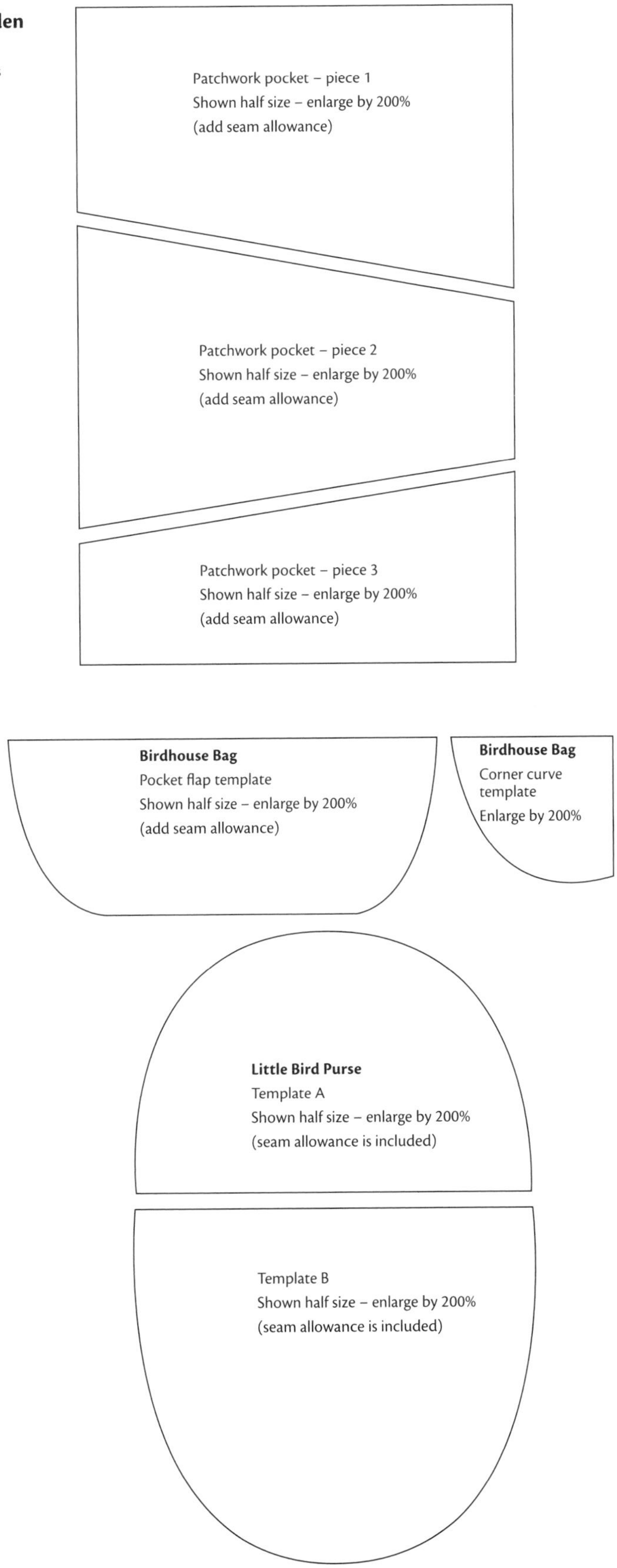

Patchwork pocket – piece 1
Shown half size – enlarge by 200%
(add seam allowance)

Patchwork pocket – piece 2
Shown half size – enlarge by 200%
(add seam allowance)

Patchwork pocket – piece 3
Shown half size – enlarge by 200%
(add seam allowance)

**Birdhouse Bag**
Pocket flap template
Shown half size – enlarge by 200%
(add seam allowance)

**Birdhouse Bag**
Corner curve
template
Enlarge by 200%

**Little Bird Purse**
Template A
Shown half size – enlarge by 200%
(seam allowance is included)

Template B
Shown half size – enlarge by 200%
(seam allowance is included)

## Walnut Tree Sewing Case

Appliqué and stitchery positions
Shown half size – enlarge by 200%

Red lines indicate appliqué placement
Black lines indicate stitchery lines
Blue lines indicate surface stitchery on appliqué

## Walnut Tree Sewing Case

Appliqué templates
Shown half size – enlarge by 200%

- - - - - indicates an area that will be under
another piece of appliqué
If using needle-turn appliqué add ¼in (6mm)
seam allowance all round
If using fusible web appliqué the templates
will need to be reversed

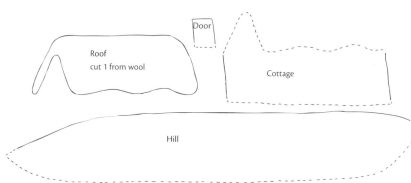

Door

Roof
cut 1 from wool

Cottage

Hill

## Walnut Tree Sewing Case

Sewing templates
Shown half size – enlarge by 200%

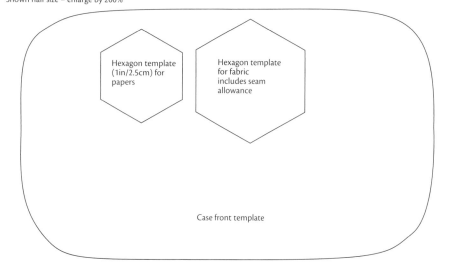

Hexagon template
(1in/2.5cm) for
papers

Hexagon template
for fabric
includes seam
allowance

Case back template

Case front template

## Walnut Tree Cottage

**Cottage Needle Holder**

Appliqué and stitchery positions

Shown half size – enlarge by 200%

Red lines indicate appliqué placement

Black lines indicate stitchery lines

Blue lines indicate surface stitchery on appliqué

## Cottage Needle Holder

Appliqué templates

Shown half size – enlarge by 200%

----------- indicates an area that will be under another piece of appliqué

If using needle-turn appliqué add ¼in (6mm) seam allowance all round

If using fusible web appliqué the templates will need to be reversed

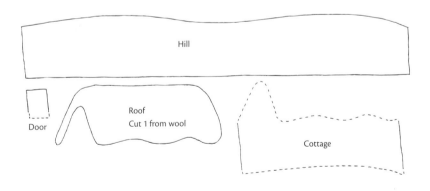

## Flowers for the Bees

**Busy Bees Wall Hanging**
Cat appliqué template
Shown half size – enlarge by 200%

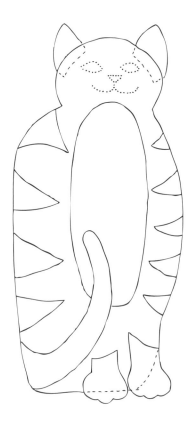

**Beehive Picture**
Stitchery design
Shown half size – enlarge by 200%

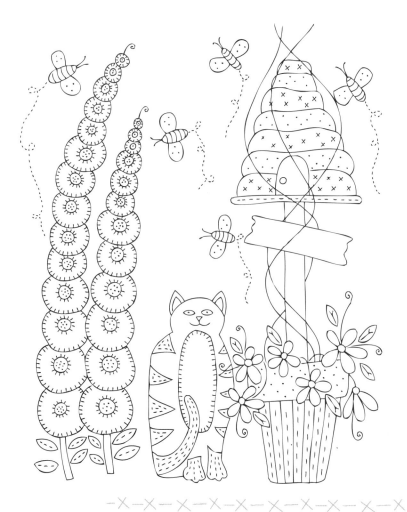

**Busy Bees Wall Hanging**
Appliqué and stitchery templates (Part 1)
Shown half size – enlarge by 200%

solid line indicates
tracing line

– – – dashed line indicates
tracing line that will be
behind another fabric

· · · · · dotted line indicates
embroidery details

(oo) place button here

ℓ stitch French knot

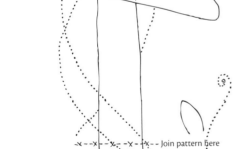

Join pattern here

Leaves – make 6

Stems – make 2

Bee – make 5

**Busy Bee Wall Hanging**
Yoyo templates
Shown half size – enlarge by 200%

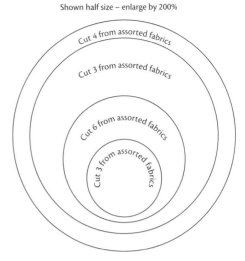

Cut 4 from assorted fabrics

Cut 3 from assorted fabrics

Cut 6 from assorted fabrics

Cut 3 from assorted fabrics

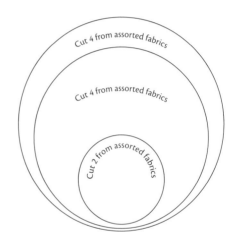

Cut 4 from assorted fabrics

Cut 4 from assorted fabrics

Cut 2 from assorted fabrics

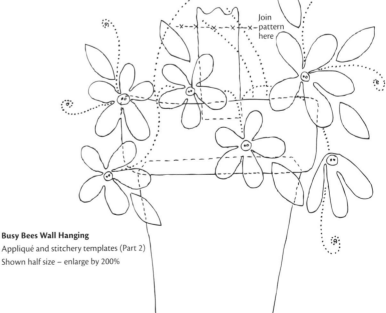

Join
pattern
here

**Busy Bees Wall Hanging**
Appliqué and stitchery templates (Part 2)
Shown half size – enlarge by 200%

## My Favourite Garden

**Garden Scenes Quilt**

**Block 1** – stitchery design

Actual size

**Block 1** – appliqué templates (shown actual size)
Trace and cut out these shapes to use as templates,
remembering to add a seam allowance if required

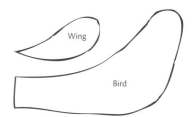

Wing

Bird

**Block 1** – surface stitchery

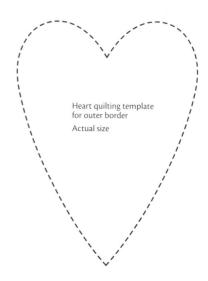

841 (BS)

844 (BS)

841 (RS)

413 (BS)

413 (FK)

839 (BS)

3860 (SS)

413 (FK)   839 (BS)

926
(BS)

844 (FK)

839 (RS)

642 (BS)

926 (BS)

926 (SS)

839
(BS)

839 (BS)

642
(LD)

841 (RS)

926 (FK)

413
(FK)

642 (LD)

**Block 1** – stitchery colour guide

Code numbers refer to DMC stranded cotton colours

**Stitch Key**

BS – backstitch

FK – French knot

LD – Lazy daisy

RS – Running stitch

SS – Satin stitch

BKS – Blanket stitch

Heart quilting template
for outer border

Actual size

## My Favourite Garden

**Garden Scenes Quilt**

**Block 2** – stitchery design

Actual size

**Block 2** – appliqué templates

(shown actual size)

Trace and cut out these shapes use as templates, remembering to add a seam allowance if required

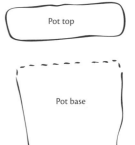

Pot top

Pot base

**Block 2** – surface stitchery

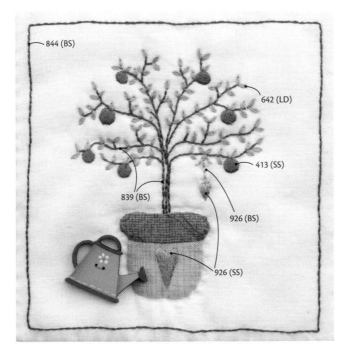

**Block 2** – stitchery colour guide

Code numbers refer to DMC stranded cotton colours

See stitch key with Block 1

## My Favourite Garden
**Garden Scenes Quilt**
**Block 3** – stitchery design
Actual size

**Block 3** – appliqué templates (shown actual size)
Trace and cut out these shapes to use as templates, remembering to add a seam allowance if required

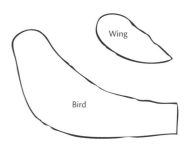

**Block 3** – surface stitchery

**Block 3** – stitchery colour guide
Code numbers refer to DMC stranded cotton colours
See stitch key with Block 1

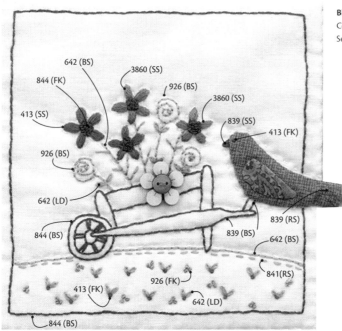

**My Favourite Garden**
**Garden Scenes Quilt**
**Block 4** – stitchery design
Actual size

**Block 4** – appliqué templates
(shown actual size)
Trace and cut out these shapes to use as templates,
remembering to add a seam allowance if required

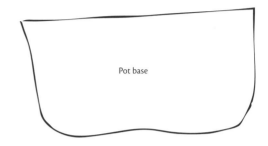

Pot top

Pot base

**Block 4** – surface stitchery

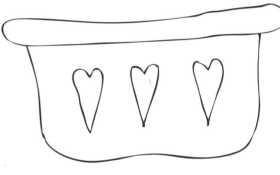

**Block 4** – stitchery colour guide
Code numbers refer to DMC stranded cotton colours
See stitch key with Block 1

## My Favourite Garden
**Garden Scenes Quilt**
**Block 5** – stitchery design
Actual size

**Block 5** – appliqué templates (shown actual size)
Trace and cut out these shapes to use as templates, remembering to add a seam allowance if required

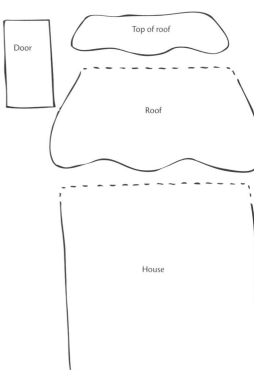

Door

Top of roof

Roof

House

**Block 5** – stitchery colour guide
Code numbers refer to DMC stranded cotton colours
See stitch key with Block 1

839 (BS)

844 (BS)

3860 (CS)

3860 (RS)

413 (BS)
926 (SS)

3860 (BS)

926 (BS)

839 (BS)

841 (RS)

413 (FK)

926 (LD)

926 (FK)

**Block 5** – surface stitchery

## My Favourite Garden

**Garden Scenes Quilt**

**Block 6** – stitchery design

Actual size

Pot top

Pot base

Pot top

Pot base

**Block 6** – stitchery colour guide

Code numbers refer to DMC stranded cotton colours

See stitch key with Block 1

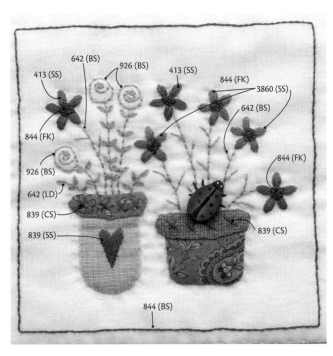

**Block 6** – surface stitchery

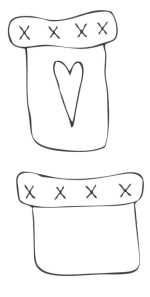

**My Favourite Garden**
**Garden Scenes Quilt**
**Block 7** – stitchery design
Actual size

Block 7 – appliqué templates (shown actual size)
Trace and cut out these shapes to use as templates,
remembering to add a seam allowance if required

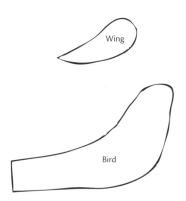

Wing

Bird

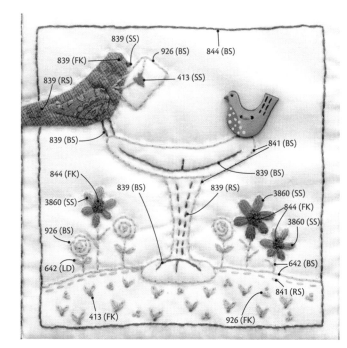

**Block 7** – stitchery colour guide
Code numbers refer to DMC stranded cotton colours
See stitch key with Block 1

**Block 7** – surface stitchery

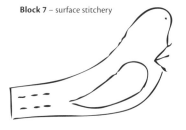

## My Favourite Garden
**Garden Scenes Quilt**
**Block 8** – stitchery design
Actual size

**Block 8** – appliqué templates (shown actual size)
Trace and cut out these shapes to use as templates, remembering to add a seam allowance if required

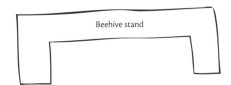

Beehive stand

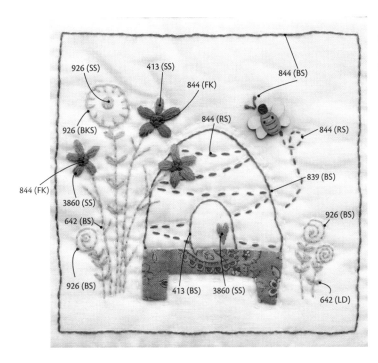

**Block 8** – stitchery colour guide
Code numbers refer to DMC stranded cotton colours
See stitch key with Block 1

## My Favourite Garden
**Garden Scenes Quilt**
**Block 9** – stitchery design
Actual size

**Block 9** – appliqué templates (shown actual size)
Trace and cut out these shapes to use as templates,
remembering to add a seam allowance if required

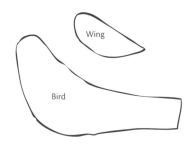

**Block 9** – surface stitchery

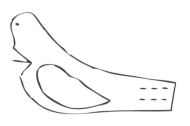

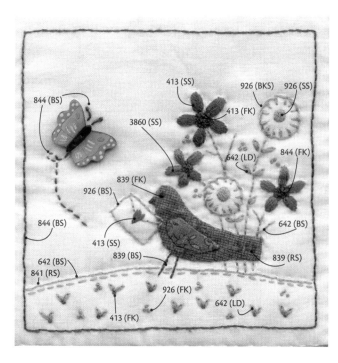

**Block 9** – stitchery colour guide
Code numbers refer to DMC stranded cotton colours
See stitch key with Block 1

−✕−✕−✕−✕−✕−✕−✕−✕−✕−✕−✕−✕−✕−✕

## My Favourite Garden

**Flowerpot Pictures – Single Pot Picture**

Stitchery colour guide

Code numbers refer to DMC
stranded cotton colours

**Stitch Key**

BS – backstitch

FK – French knot

LD – Lazy daisy

RS – Running stitch

SS – Satin stitch

BKS – Blanket stitch

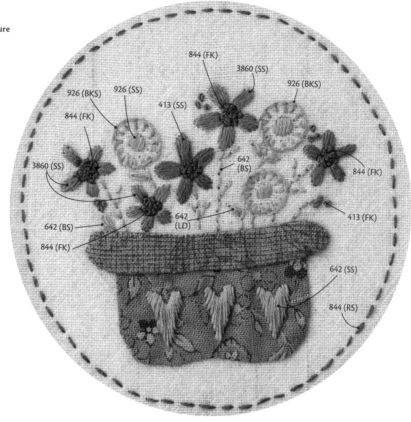

**Two Pots Picture**

Stitchery colour guide

Code numbers refer to DMC
stranded cotton colours

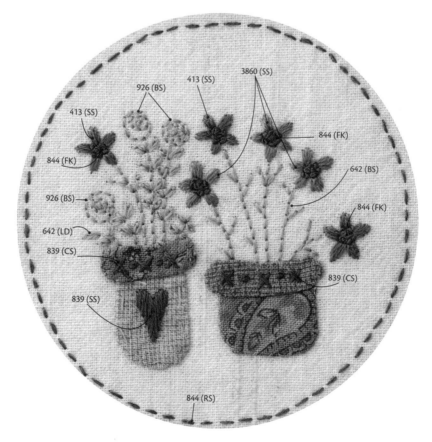

## Go Wild Garden

### Go Wild Quilt

Appliqué templates and surface stitchery design

Actual size

———— indicates tracing line

– – – – indicates tracing line
that will be behind another fabric

........ indicates details to be embroidered

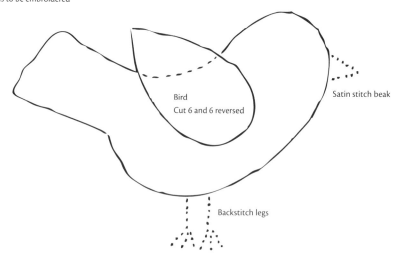

Bird
Cut 6 and 6 reversed

Satin stitch beak

Backstitch legs

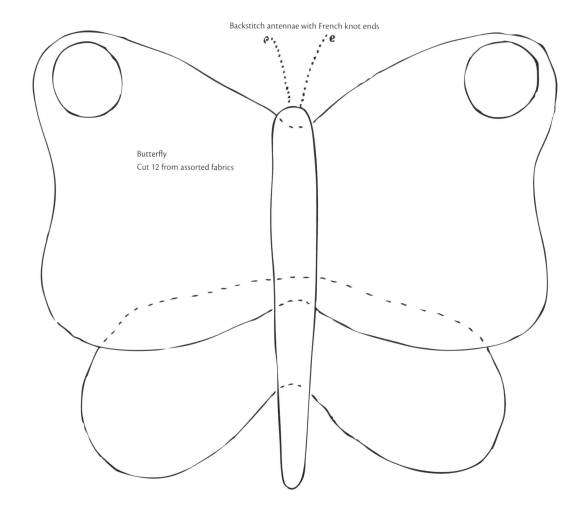

Backstitch antennae with French knot ends

Butterfly
Cut 12 from assorted fabrics

**Go Wild Quilt**

Appliqué templates

Actual size

Watering can
Cut 6 and 6 reversed from assorted fabrics

Heart

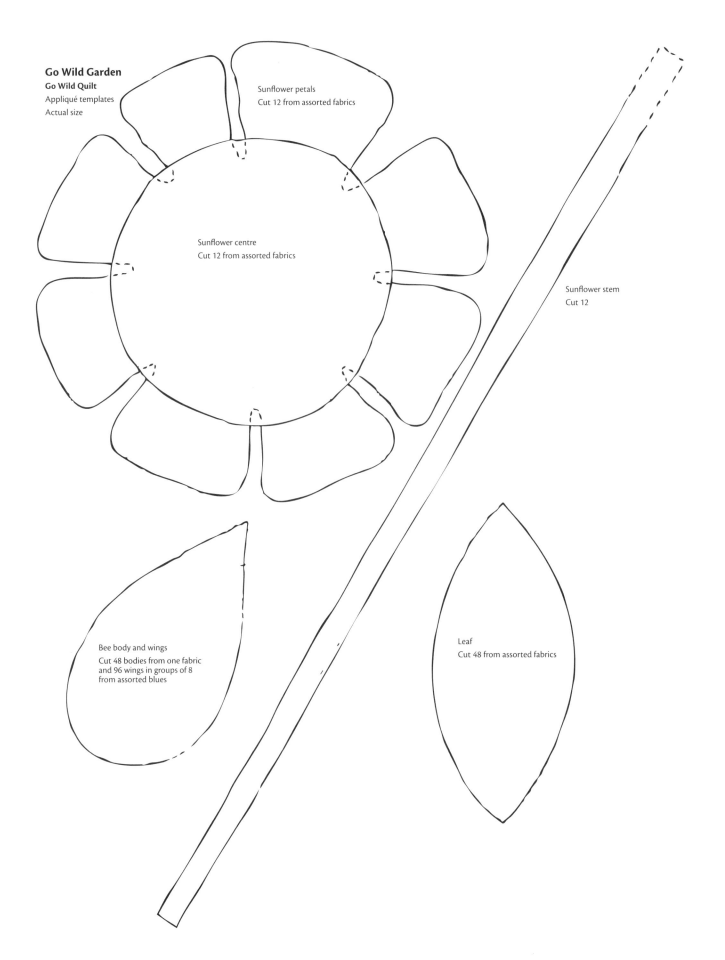

**Go Wild Garden**
**Go Wild Quilt**
Appliqué templates
Actual size

Sunflower petals
Cut 12 from assorted fabrics

Sunflower centre
Cut 12 from assorted fabrics

Sunflower stem
Cut 12

Bee body and wings
Cut 48 bodies from one fabric
and 96 wings in groups of 8
from assorted blues

Leaf
Cut 48 from assorted fabrics

**Go Wild Quilt**

Border quilting template

Actual size

To achieve a repeating border quilting pattern, position and mark the template as shown here. Move the template along the border as needed to complete the pattern all round

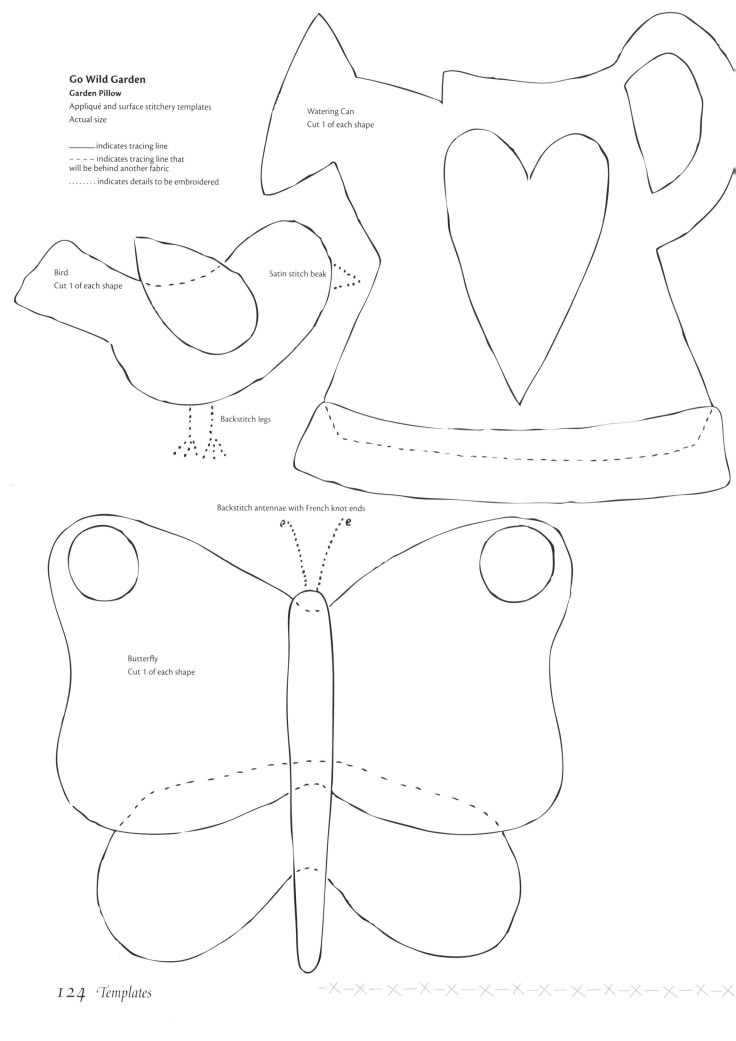

**Go Wild Garden**

**Garden Pillow**
Appliqué and surface stitchery templates
Actual size

——— indicates tracing line
– – – – indicates tracing line that
will be behind another fabric
........ indicates details to be embroidered

Watering Can
Cut 1 of each shape

Bird
Cut 1 of each shape

Satin stitch beak

Backstitch legs

Backstitch antennae with French knot ends

Butterfly
Cut 1 of each shape

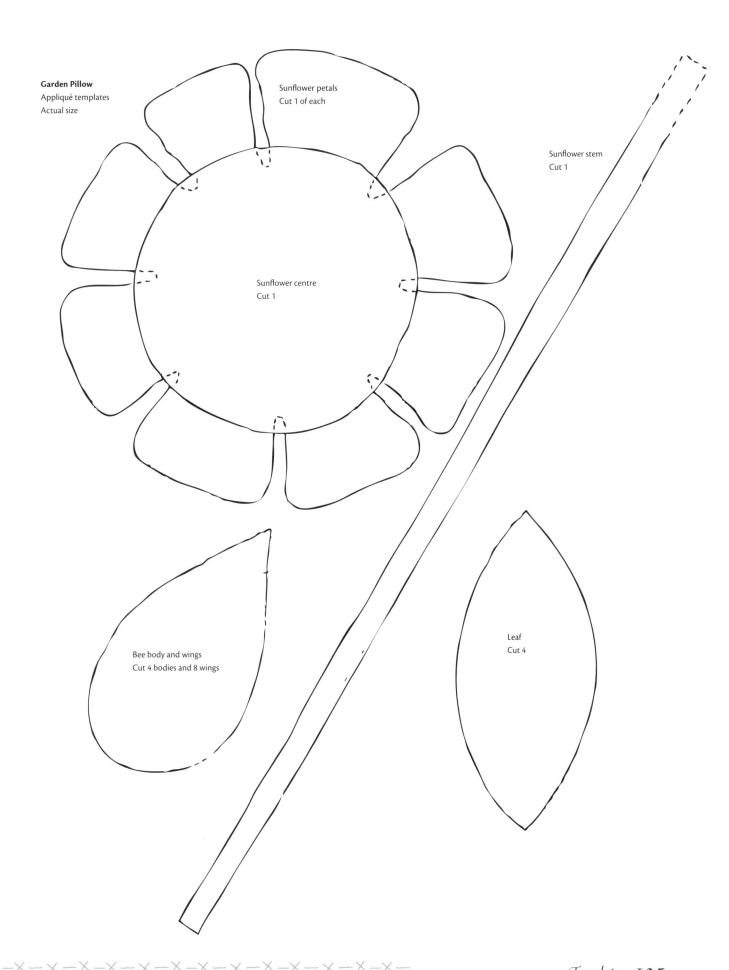

**Garden Pillow**
Appliqué templates
Actual size

Sunflower petals
Cut 1 of each

Sunflower centre
Cut 1

Sunflower stem
Cut 1

Bee body and wings
Cut 4 bodies and 8 wings

Leaf
Cut 4

# Suppliers

**Lynette Anderson Designs**

PO Box 9314, Pacific Paradise, QLD 4564, Australia

Tel: 07 5450 7497; from outside Australia +61 7 5450 7497

www.lynetteandersondesigns.com.au for all wholesale enquires regarding Lynette's patterns and books

www.lynetteandersondesigns.bigcartel.com for the sewing case used in the Walnut Tree Sewing Case and the hand-painted wooden buttons used on the Garden Scenes Quilt

Blog: www.lynetteandersondesigns.typepad.com

Twitter: @lynettestitches

**DMC Creative World Ltd**

1st Floor Compass Building, Feldspar Close, Enderby, Leicestershire LE19 4SD, UK

Tel: 0116 275 4000

Fax: 0116 275 4020

www.dmccreative.co.uk

For embroidery fabrics, stranded embroidery cottons and other embroidery supplies

**Lecien Fabrics**

5515 Doyle Street, Suite 6, Emeryville, CA 94608, USA

Tel: +1 510 596 3085

Fax: + 1 510 596 3004

Email: info@lecienusa.com

www.lecienusa.com

For fabrics, including those designed by Lynette Anderson

# About the Author

Lynette Anderson's love affair with textiles began at a young age when her grandmother taught her to embroider and knit. Patchwork caught Lynette's attention in 1981 after the birth of her first son, and her affinity with textiles is apparent in her work. Moving with her family to Australia in 1990 prompted the release of Lynette first patterns in 1995 and during the ensuing years Lynette has produced hundreds of patterns. Lynette's distinctive, yet sophisticated naïve design style encompasses quilts, pillow, bags and sewing accessories. Her popular self-published books include, *Bearly Stitched*, *Sunflower Stitching*, *An Angel's Wish*, *Friends For Christmas* and *Rainbow Cottage*. Lynette was very excited when she was asked to design fabric for Lecien with whom she launched her first line 'Summertime Friends' in 2010 with 'Scandinavian Christmas' and 'Secret Garden' following in 2011. Lynette's first book for David & Charles, *It's Quilting Cats & Dogs*, was published in 2010. Visit Lynette at www.lynetteandersondesigns.typepad.com

# Acknowledgments

Many thanks to Val – without your help I would not have finished everything in time. Your embroidery stitches match mine perfectly and your hand quilting is wonderful. To Barb, a big thank you for machine quilting the Flower Spool Quilt on such short notice. Thanks also to Emma and Lyn who work constantly in the background at Lynette Anderson Designs to ensure that I can draw and stitch without interruption on the days that I need to focus.

# Index

A DAVID & CHARLES BOOK
Copyright © David & Charles Limited 2012

David & Charles is an imprint of F&W Media International, Ltd
Brunel House, Forde Close, Newton Abbot, TQ12 4PU, UK

F&W Media International, Ltd is a subsidiary of F+W Media, Inc
10151 Carver Road, Suite #200, Blue Ash, OH 45242, USA

First published in the UK and US in 2012

Text and designs copyright © Lynette Anderson 2012
Layout and photography copyright © David & Charles 2012

Lynette Anderson has asserted her right to be identified as author of this
work in accordance with the Copyright, Designs and Patents Act, 1988.

All rights reserved. No part of this publication may be reproduced,
stored in a retrieval system, or transmitted, in any form or by any
means, electronic or mechanical, by photocopying, recording or
otherwise, without prior permission in writing from the publisher.

Readers are permitted to reproduce any of the patterns or
designs in this book for their personal use and without the
prior permission of the publisher. However, the designs in this
book are copyright and must not be reproduced for resale.

The author and publisher have made every effort to ensure
that all the instructions in the book are accurate and safe, and
therefore cannot accept liability for any resulting injury, damage
or loss to persons or property, however it may arise.

Names of manufacturers, fabric ranges and other products
are provided for the information of readers, with no
intention to infringe copyright or trademarks.

A catalogue record for this book is available from the British Library.

ISBN-13: 978-1-4463-0039-8
ISBN-10: 1-4463-0039-0

Printed in China by RR Donnelley
for F&W Media International, LTD
Brunel House, Newton Abbot, Devon

Publisher  Alison Myer
Acquisitions Editor  Sarah Callard
Desk Editor  James Brooks
Project Editor  Lin Clements
Art Editor  Charly Bailey
Photographers  Vanessa Davies & Lorna Yabsley
Senior Production Controller  Kelly Smith

F&W Media International, LTD publishes high quality books on a wide
range of subjects. For more great book ideas visit: www.stitchcraftcreate.co.uk

To my dear husband Vince,
who encourages me every
day and thinks each new
project is 'the best' I have
ever done! Thank you for
always being there and for
encouraging me to keep
creating.